D1585027

Three Scottish Colourists

Three
Scottish Colourists

S. J. PEPLOE ★ F. C. B. CADELL
LESLIE HUNTER

T. J. HONEYMAN

Thomas Nelson and Sons Ltd
London Edinburgh Paris Melbourne Toronto
and New York

THOMAS NELSON AND SONS LTD

Parkside Works Edinburgh 9
3 Henrietta Street London WC2
312 Flinders Street Melbourne C1
5 Parker's Buildings Burg Street Cape Town

THOMAS NELSON AND SONS (CANADA) LTD
91–93 Wellington Street West   Toronto 1

THOMAS NELSON AND SONS
385 Madison Avenue New York 17

SOCIÉTÉ FRANÇAISE D'EDITIONS NELSON
25 rue Henri Barbusse Paris Vᵉ

———

First published August 1950

The text of this book is set in
12 point Baskerville

Preface

THIS book is a joint effort. Apart from printers and publishers who have served us well, this is a collaboration between Ion Harrison and myself. We have long held the view that, notwithstanding the very clear and definite indications of a growing appreciation, an effort should be made to make the work of Peploe, Hunter and Cadell even more widely known to a larger public. But it is intended to be something more than a memorial tribute. The guiding motive rests on convictions arrived at during their lifetime. It is, in a sense, an apology for the national feebleness in critical understanding of pictorial art values, and if the argument is not convincing, at least no-one is hurt.

The idea of building the book, so to speak, round one collection of paintings has its obvious advantages. Ion Harrison has, over a number of years, concentrated on acquiring a comprehensive range of works by each of the artists. He continues to do so on the principle that one cannot have too much of a good thing. His collection includes paintings by other artists, but some years ago he decided, principally for his own pleasure, but also under a compelling sense of admiration, to specialise in these three Scottish colourists. For several reasons, therefore—some of which will probably emerge in the text—the collector and the writer have united in the preparation of this volume, sustained by the hope that the artists themselves will—through their works—speak for themselves.

v

Acknowledgments

I HAVE to place on record my thanks to the following for assisting in the preparation of this book : Mrs Peploe, Mrs Percival Clark (Miss Jean Cadell), Mrs Robert Trail Rose, Miss Isabel Mackintosh, Miss Anne Hill, Mrs Johnston, Mr J. D. Fergusson, Mr Stanley Cursiter, Mr Rupert Roddam, and the authors and publishers of books mentioned in the text.

T. J. H.

Contents

INTRODUCTION

    General and Polemical   1

    The Scottish Tradition   12

    Three Scottish Colourists   35

S. J. PEPLOE   47

F. C. B. CADELL   71

LESLIE HUNTER   93

AS I REMEMBER THEM

    by Ion R. Harrison   117

INDEX   127

S. J. Peploe 1871–1935

COLOUR PLATES

I	Roses and Fruit on Table	52
II	Benmhor, Mull, from Iona	56
III	Roses and Still Life	56–7
IV	Boats at Royan	60
V	Trees, Antibes	64
VI	Roses and Fruit	64–5

BLACK AND WHITE PLATES
(between pages 68 and 69)

1 Head of a Boy

2 Melon, Grapes and Apples

3 Loaf and Jug

4 Roses in China Vase

5 The Pine Trees

6 Tulips

7 Street in Cassis

8 Street Scene, France

Photograph of S. J. Peploe with Willy and Denis   48

F. C. B. Cadell 1883–1937

COLOUR PLATES

I	The White Room	76
II	Port Bhan, Iona	80
III	Mrs Ion R. Harrison	80–1
IV	The Harbour, Cassis	84
V	Interior, Croft House	88

BLACK AND WHITE PLATES
(between pages 92 and 93)

1 The Pink Azaleas

2 Reflections

3 The Sacristy Door, Iona

4 The West Highlands, Sound of Mull

5 The Drawing Room, Croft House

6 Iona Farm

7 (*left*) The Boxers   (*right*) The Biplane

8 (*left*) In Hospital   (*right*) The Two Jocks

Photograph of F. C. B. Cadell   72

Leslie Hunter 1879–1931

COLOUR PLATES

I	Chrysanthemums	100
II	The Storm, Largo	104
III	The Malacca Cane	104–5
	(Portrait of Duncan Macdonald Esq.)	
IV	St Paul	108
V	House-boats, Balloch	112

BLACK AND WHITE PLATES
(between pages 116 and 117)

1   Fife Village

2   Boats, Loch Lomond

3   Roses in Glass Vase

4   Lobster on Blue Plate

5   Interior with Figure

6   The Harbour, Villefranche

7   (*left*) The Clock Tower, Venice
     (*right*) Interior of French Church

8   (*upper*) Fife Cottage
     (*lower*) Rotten Row, Hyde Park, London

Photograph of Leslie Hunter   94

Introduction

GENERAL AND POLEMICAL

NOTWITHSTANDING the observations of Whistler and others that Art might be received in silence, I still cling to the view that on occasion it is appropriate and helpful to say something about it.

This introduction may appear at first glance to be only remotely related to the main purpose of the book. Nevertheless, it seems necessary to me that we should supply a historical background, discuss the effects of contemporary criticism on both artist and spectator, examine the reasons which lead one to group Peploe, Hunter and Cadell under the title *Three Scottish Colourists* and investigate the claim that pictorial Art in Scotland is not as negligible as some people at home and abroad appear to think.

Thinking about Art is not confined to one place or time, but talking and writing about it tends to become focused on period and location. In Britain the centre is London. Speaking generally the worth of any past or contemporary contribution made by artists who elect to live and work elsewhere in the United Kingdom has to be assessed according to standards created by critics and amateurs in London. This, of course, appears to be all wrong to those who are anxious to keep Scots artists in Scotland for Scotland's sake.

Frequently in their lifetime Peploe, Hunter and Cadell were urged to make their headquarters in London. Just before his untimely death Hunter had decided to move there and had actually acquired a studio. London had no attractions for Peploe. The social conventions and way of life in art circles as he saw them were enough to convince him of

I

an incompatability which he would be unable to overcome. Cadell would have fitted in with the greatest of ease, and in all likelihood would have made himself an outstanding figure, perhaps an inheritor of the gay nineties tradition in social brilliance. Hunter, with his lovable eccentricities, Cadell, with his sparkling wit and lively conversation, would have adapted themselves to the formulae of introductions to circles which operate as honorary publicity agents. Peploe would have been miserable. Allan Ramsay and David Wilkie first made their reputations in the south. Raeburn and others tried to and failed. Some of the Glasgow School succumbed to the London pull, and in due time received high academic honours. More recently two young Scots— Colquhoun and McBride—have achieved a very considerable reputation, and are usually the sole representatives of Scotland when official bodies organise exhibitions of contemporary British Art for circulation abroad.

Scottish Nationalism

Now, there are many people in Scotland who are opposed to nationalism as a political philosophy, but who are strongly in favour of it as a cultural enterprise. They are convinced that Scotland is quite as capable of producing talent and genius in the arts as is any other part of the world. In support of this they delve deeply into history and they some-times become very critical of London or English rule. Indeed it is not unlikely that they ignore some facts that are incon-venient to the argument. A strong element of bias may emerge hereafter, but we can at least start out with this admission : in the recognition of genius, even when it is well within the range of his vision, the Scot is no more acute than other human beings. Certainly we have been, and still are, obtuse and reactionary, although we may no longer pray, 'Grant, O God! that we may always be right, for Thou knowest we will never change our minds.'

It would be ridiculous to claim for Scotland a high place

in the international field of art production, but we have produced artists who were unquestionably entitled to a place in the history of British Art greater than has been granted to them. Most contemporary publications, exhibitions, talks and articles carrying the general title of British Art should be more properly termed English Art, because of the almost complete absence of reference to native resident Scottish artists. The fault lies in ourselves. It has often been said that if Scottish Art had been entitled to a more prominent place in the histories of British Art it would have won it without any difficulty. The assumption is that fame and distinction are made solely on merit. This is not so. If the arts are to be sustained in a flourishing condition they must be continually refreshed in the hearts and minds of the people. And any enterprise, whether it be on the lines of writing, talking, explaining, etc. which has this in view, should be freed from obstructions lying in its path.

Books on Art and artists are numerous enough, but relatively few deal with Scottish Art and artists. There are probably many reasons to explain this dearth of literature ; one of them is that we appear to have lost the sound critical faculty which, at one time, was accepted as a feature of Scottish comment on Art and Letters. We have grown apologetic. Somehow or other we appear to think it is bad taste, or undignified to publicise our novelists, dramatists and painters. In England and France it is otherwise.

Let me intrude a personal experience. Some time ago I was asked to contribute to an important volume on Scotland. The purpose of the book, I was led to believe, was to make the various aspects of national life in Scotland more widely known abroad. I was honoured by the invitation to write about art galleries and art, and I thought it well to prepare a factual account of recent evidence that Scottish artists were becoming increasingly better known abroad. In illustration thereof, I quoted the experience of a distinguished visitor from Australia, a director of an art gallery, who had remarked

3

that in the course of a few days' visit to Edinburgh and Glasgow he had seen more of interest in the realm of pictorial art than he had seen in London in the preceding three or four weeks. To prove that this was something more than a courteous observation, he acquired, for shipment to Australia, three or four works by young Scottish artists. I was, however, instructed to eliminate this information, and I am still puzzled to know the reason why. I cannot refrain from adding a sentence spoken to me in London shortly before the war by the well-known French artist Dunoyer de Segonzac. ' You are a strange people you English.' [He meant British.] ' Hunter is one of your great painters and nobody knows anything about him.' By the same token it is fitting to note that Mr Stanley Cursiter recalls hearing Oscar Kokoscha, the eminent Czech artist, say in front of W. Y. Macgregor's *Vegetable Stall*, ' To think that that picture was painted before I was born and I never knew.'

Criticism and Educational Methods

Much of what stands today for criticism is more concerned with the failings than with the excellences of a young artist. A perusal of the available ' notices ' directed for or against the work of Peploe, Hunter and Cadell at various stages in their careers is more than interesting. It is revealing. It is not difficult to produce evidence in support of the opinion that criticism seems to have taken the wrong turning. Let it be granted that the critic has his own rights as an artist, and that the work of others serves him as the raw material for demonstrating his own capacity as a critic. But it is clear that not enough consideration is given to the immediate effect of ill-natured or ill-informed comment. There is no comfort or solace for the artist in the conviction that posterity will take a more enlightened view because it will accept the faults as the price that must be paid for the qualities.

There will always be critics of any production by the hand of man. Whether in the long run they serve any useful purpose is an argument which does not belong here. That the professionally employed critics have influence is unquestionable. They supply us with the phrases which we use in the course of polite, or impolite, conversation on the Arts. I know from experience how hurtful or helpful an observation or critical comment in a newspaper or journal can be in determining the success or otherwise of an art exhibition. I know, too, how immeasurable is my debt to writers on every aspect of art appreciation and history. Speaking of history we know that it is full of evidence of young and not so young artists, who languished for want of encouragement.

But the argument rests on something more than inadequate or inefficient criticism. It goes back to the deficiencies in our educational system. We have ignored to a great extent the value of training and discipline in the development of an emotional outlook. It is only in recent years that art and the history and appreciation of art have been given a place in the day-school curriculum. And, with the exception of Edinburgh, the universities entirely ignore art as an essential in cultural training or as fundamental to a liberal education. Glasgow has now appointed a whole-time lecturer in the History of Art, but there is still no collective functioning between the various educational bodies. There is an absence of continuity for those students who elect to take Art as a subject in the School Leaving Certificate examination. The examination questions on Art Appreciation for this certificate are admirable, but there is little or no evidence that the actual productions of the artists which have been the subject of study are ever seriously considered. One does not teach the appreciation of drama or poetry without, at least, reading the works of playwrights and poets. Furthermore, there is growing support for the idea that if the pupil cannot be made to see *Macbeth* as a play he should not be compelled to read it. The appreciation of the pictorial arts will always tend to be a dry and dusty detached study unless the vitally essential supplement, i.e. the productions—preferably the originals—can be made available.

The availability of originals raises another question of some importance in educational matters other than that of art appreciation, especially since I have asserted that the fault lies in ourselves. In February 1948 *The Scotsman* printed an important article entitled ' Scottish Studies,' the first sentence of which read : ' It is a common complaint that the state of Scottish studies is unsatisfactory : that they are inadequately encouraged, even by the universities, and that insufficient research is done.' The subsequent arguments, related to the lamentable neglect of Scottish records, and the several suggestions were cordially received by a number of correspondents representing varied interests.

The inadequacy of the financial provisions is a political matter which will, we hope, be attended to in due course, but it is by no means the complete explanation.

I indict the scholars and historians for their obscurantism. The history of our country has been too much regarded as the special property of those who have been initiated into the mysteries of documents and records. The modern methods of visual education have been ignored. We have failed to stimulate the imagination and the intellect of our young—and not so young—students who should have become better informed about and received inspiration from their cultural heritage. Let me give one concrete example.

Some time ago I was encouraged by the Right Honourable Tom Johnston to look into the matter of *The Declaration of Arbroath*. He led me to the discovery that a great many people, including university graduates, had either never heard of *The Declaration of Arbroath* or had retained only the vaguest idea of what it was about. On discussing the matter with educationists who specialised in teaching Scottish History they expressed surprise at the reports of such widespread ignorance. The subject, they said, was constantly referred to in school classroom, university lecture courses and on the air. The answer then became clear. People do not remember the importance and significance of this great historical document because they have never seen it. Acting on this hypothesis an attempt was made to borrow the original document for exhibition in the Glasgow Art Gallery. It was planned to do this with an organised publicity campaign, bringing the school children of all ages to see it and generally to mark the occasion in a big way. Repeated applications met with failure. It would establish a dangerous precedent we were told—in an age when precedents are being created almost daily. It would subject a rare and valuable document to grave risks—when for the last twenty-five years risks have been taken with great and irreplaceable works of art of international fame.

No enterprise is without risk these days, but the risks have to be measured against the benefits. Now, this is not an attack on those to whom the preservation of historical documents of great rarity and of priceless value is entrusted. This country is especially fortunate in the custodians of its treasures—they are men of integrity and of knowledge, fully aware of their responsibilities. But it is surely fair to argue that our failure to achieve the full results of a sound, liberal education, which will ensure the creation of a proper patriotism in the cultural sense (and that includes the creative arts), is owing to our short-sightedness and unwillingness to take risks which are, after all, negligible almost to the point of non-existence. *The Declaration of Arbroath* is not even locked in a safe. It lies framed, protected by glass, on a table in the Register House in Edinburgh. It is accessible to any visitor, who will be courteously received. In this respect, therefore, you have to ask for visual education. It will certainly not be thrust upon you.

Dearth of Literature

Inasmuch, therefore, as a work of art may not come to life until it is confronted by a spectator, so is it unlikely that a full measure of appreciation will be accorded to the artist

7

unless something is known about him. For most of us the biographical details are of interest only if they have some bearing on the artist's work—and I shall try to keep that in mind in the subsequent parts of this book. But, remembering that the number of people in Scotland to whom one could apply the description ' art lover ' is lamentably small, it is necessary to animadvert on the importance of a vital and up-to-date literature.

Ramsay, Raeburn, Wilkie are names to be found in any ordinary dictionary of art written in the English language. Of these three probably Raeburn has had most written about his work. I know of no book devoted to the life of Ramsay, although Sir James Caw has a long and interesting article in the *Proceedings of the Walpole Society*. With the exception of Alan Cunningham's indifferent book, nothing of any real importance on Wilkie has appeared. (A new work is projected and it is being written by an American !) Of the three general histories on Scottish painting up to the beginning of World War I, that by Sir James Caw, published in 1908, is the only one worthy of serious attention. Recently Mr Stanley Cursiter has written a fresh survey covering the period from the earliest authentic work to the end of last century. Other writers, notably Mr Ian Finlay, have also produced some very valuable contributions. But a great deal of original research and fresh analyses in the light of contemporary thought still remains to be done. The Glasgow School won an international reputation but achieved only two very slight literary essays (both forty years ago) by way of complement. It is certain that if the group had operated from London or Paris a considerable list of publications would have marked the movement.

There appears to be no doubt regarding the value of publications—of various kinds—in stimulating interest in art. Memoirs of Hunter and Peploe have certainly made more people curious about their work in particular and about the theory and practice of art in general.

Art Appreciation

It would, however, be foolish to ignore the fact that there is a body of opinion which holds that lectures, discussions, essays, memoirs and biographies and all other attempts to make people ' understand ' art are misdirected and futile. This view is given some support by a recent utterance from Sir Alfred Munnings, past President of the Royal Academy : ' If you want to judge a picture let the man on the dockside see it. Let the miner see it. I would rather take their opinion. Those men in the street are the best judges.' It is not easy to reconcile this with the opinion of the first president of the Royal Academy : ' Taste does not come by chance or nature ; it is a long and laborious business to acquire it. It is the lowest style only of Art that may be said, in the vulgar sense, to be naturally pleasing.'

That brings one right up against the procedure followed in various institutions charged with the duty of ' bringing art to the people.' In our art galleries and museums we have no written constitutions, but I quote Mr Francis Henry Taylor, the Director of the Metropolitan Museum, New York, who records that in the original programme of his building it was stated : ' The purpose is to afford to our whole people free and ample means for innocent and refined enjoyment, and also supplying the best facilities for practical instruction and for the cultivation of pure taste in all matters connected with the arts.'

Have we failed to do this ? Have we placed Art beyond the reach of the man in the street ? Is it not the case that instead of breaking down the barriers which separate him from the ' greatness ' in works of art and from the delights of real appreciation, we assail him with words and phrases like ' significant and plastic form,' ' harmonious design,' ' fine feeling for line or paint,' ' orchestrations of colour,' ' linear arabesques and conceits ' and so on. He calls it jargon or mumbo-jumbo. The very word ' aesthetics ' terrifies him, and he seeks protection by arming himself with the weapons of ridicule or leaves the field to the ' high-brow.' He explains aesthetics thus : ' When you see and hear two people talking in front of a picture, and if the one who is listening doesn't understand what the other fellow is talking about, and the one who is talking doesn't understand himself, that's aesthetics ! '

Now we know that it isn't jargon or mumo-jumbo. Contemporary writers and teachers use the nomenclature of the science of perception, i.e. aesthetics. They use words and phrases and analogies which are quite comprehensible to those of us who have taken the trouble to learn the language. Nevertheless, we, whose job it is to ' show ' works of art have no right to demand the full aesthetic equipment from the sincere seeker after enlightenment or to insult him if he, timidly and apologetically, explains, ' I know nothing about Art—I like this or that picture, but I don't know why.'

On the one side, therefore, you have the Munnings school of thought which assumes that the only barrier to a sound appreciation of the arts is a state of total blindness, more or less. On the other there is the Common-Sense school, a title borrowed from the Scottish School of Philosophy which flourished in the eighteenth century. And we quote from one of its creators, Thomas Reid (1710–96), Professor of Philosophy at Glasgow University : ' A work of art may appear beautiful to the most ignorant—even to a child—but to one who understands it perfectly and perceives how every part of it is fitted with exact judgment to its end, the beauty is not mysterious, it is perfectly comprehended : and he knows wherein it exists, as well as how it affects him.' Or, in other words—those of Bishop Berkeley—' It is therefore one thing to see an object and another to discern its beauty.' This is not the place to carry this discussion further. It is introduced because of its bearing on one's own development in art appreciation, especially with regard to the three artists under consideration.

I recall my first contact with the work of S. J. Peploe.

It was at the time when he appeared to have switched his allegiance from the Impressionists and had begun to apprehend and act upon the new uses of colour as developed by Cézanne and others. I confess that it was quite beyond me. Nothing that he then produced could measure up to the standards of what I had been taught or had experienced. Similarly with Hunter. Cadell's work was then unknown to me. Not until I had succeeded in stepping over from the conception that a painting must conform to *my ideas* concerning subject and treatment, to the more humble, more polite and infinitely more correct understanding that the spectator has to contemplate an *artist's idea*, did I begin to know what it was all about.

My experience is not by any means unique, but the fact still remains that none of these three Scottish colourists can yet be looked upon, in the ordinary sense, as popular painters. Are any worthwhile artists ever popular ? Hugh MacDiarmid answers it in these lines :

> Are my poems spoken in the factories and fields,
> In the streets o' the toon ?
> Gin they're no', then I'm failin' to dae
> What I ocht to ha' dune.
>
> Gin I canna win through to the man in the street,
> The wife by the hearth,
> A' the cleverness on earth 'll no' mak' up
> For the damnable dearth.
>
> Haud on, haud on ; what poet's dune that ?
> Is Shakespeare read,
> Or Dante or Milton or Goethe or Burns ?
> —You heard what I said.

Nor does it follow that the accepted, in so-called informed art circles, are universally acknowledged as having played any very important part in British Art. Witness two fairly recent comments. First, *The Scotsman's* critic on Ian Finlay's book *Art in Scotland* (1948) : ' The truth is that Mr Finlay accepts the fashionable idea that Peploe and Leslie Hunter are our greatest and most typical modern painters, whereas it is probably the case that the cities of the world abound in French-inspired eclectics like these.' That is a fairly-stated opinion and it merits investigation which will come later. Then second, *The Times Literary Supplement* dealing with Stanley Cursiter's *Peploe* (1948) : ' In particular it was surely a mistake to attempt as Peploe often did, a very direct imitation of the style of Cézanne ; his facility, the one gift that Cézanne did not possess, led him always to take a short cut where Cézanne took a long one, and the result is that the master's handling is often reduced to a trick and the forms inexpressively simplified by means of a borrowed formula.' Here again is an opinion which calls for discussion in due course. The immediate point is that each of these adverse views is related to influences which the writers believe are discernible in the works of the artists we are considering. Therefore, before particularising on the personal contribution of each, we ought to examine the historical backgrounds first of all from a national aspect and then from the beginning of the ' modern movement ' in painting.

THE SCOTTISH TRADITION

As far as we know, no-one has yet found a satisfactory answer to questions such as these : ' What determines a nation's superlative achievements in particular branches of the Fine Arts ? ' ' Why is Italian Painting of the fourteenth and fifteenth centuries great art ? Dutch and Spanish in their turn, and French in the nineteenth, and, so far, in the twentieth ? ' Climate, temperament, religion, tradition and other factors have been offered, but the exceptions are as numerous as the agreements and the question remains unanswered.

Puritanical Scale of Values

It has often been said that a ' puritanical scale of values ' destroyed any chances that Scottish Art—and to a lesser extent English Art—might have had to make itself universally great and significant. If John Knox had remained and died a prisoner on a French galley, if the Reformation had not been imported, if the ' art treasures ' in the abbeys and churches had not been destroyed so wantonly, culture, and especially the Fine Arts might have had a chance. And so on. Of course, the Reformation and its doctrine that art was essentially immoral must have played havoc with art activities, full grown and embryonic, but only for a time. Human nature can be changed more by religion than by any other single force, but in no country have theological doctrines and injunctions ever seeped right through into the heart of a people with anything more than transient results. The reaction is inevitable. How else can one explain David Hume, the Allan Ramsays, father and son, Burns and Carlyle? The Inquisition did not prevent Spain from producing her greatest artists and poets in the period of her greatest oppression. Apart from that, it is very doubtful if the Reformation in Scotland did, by itself, exercise a stranglehold on any intellectual or cultural urge.

However much we feel like making Calvinism a scapegoat for our lack of great achievement in the arts, we can pass from the argument by agreeing that art is not the whole of life, that there are other national issues with a historical background. Our detractors admit that the Bronze and Iron Ages in Scotland produced as high a degree of ornamentation and decorative art as that of any other primitive races. They also surmise that the Picts were competent tattoo artists with ' modern ' tendencies, hence the walls built by the academic Romans and the institution of an Independent Salon in Caledonia !

Although it is necessary to appeal to history, we need not labour under the illusion that the right conclusion may thus be arrived at. But because of the insufficiency of any critical approach as distinct from the factual accounts (of which there are several) it is opportune to examine what we mean by the

Scottish Tradition in painting. This is attempted with considerable diffidence because of some doubts hinted at in an anecdote told by the illustrious Italian philosopher, Benedetto Croce. He tells of a student who was directed to study a volume of history dealing, hypercritically, with Ancient Rome. Some time later the student returned the book with the following remark : 'I have acquired the proud conviction of being the most learned of historians, for it appears that they arrive at the conclusion that they know nothing, as the result of exhaustive toil, while I know nothing without any effort at all, simply as a generous gift of nature.'

National Characteristics

One has heard so often of this or that painter working in the Scottish Tradition, the special characteristics of which are related to the richness of our landscape—with its great atmospheric variations—to the sense of pattern and design derived from Celtic carvings and illuminations and so on. As a result of exhaustive toil I have failed to see it. If our artists derived their inspiration from what may be described as ' national subject-matter,' then to that extent we may speak of a Scottish School of painting. But no classification of this kind can have any bearing on the contribution made to the common pool of aesthetic achievement of this age. What, therefore, beyond the nationality or residence of its creator, makes a painting qualify for inclusion in the Scottish School ? And if, in this sense, we claim a national art should not this be related to the number of artists we are willing or able to support ? An art can become national only when the people are part of it, when the thing is alive as an integral part of the social structure. And it is not yet so in Scotland.

It has been so in the crafts and in poetry and music— when these are used by the people and instinctively and emotionally felt. Painting has not responded as fully as the other arts to the cultural tendencies throughout our history. It may be because the language of paint—colour, line, space and light, etc.—has no nationality that one finds it difficult to apprehend a Scottish Tradition in painting. Or perhaps it is only when these elements are handled in a particular way *over a long period of time* that they may assume forms which can be defined as having a national quality. The evidence of Celtic Art—where subject has little or no bearing—and architecture, for obvious reasons, may lend support to the idea.

Our tradition is European. Influences from the Continent, either directly imported by foreigners or acquired by our own artists in their foreign travels, flare up, leave their mark and pass on into new developments. Scottish artists generally have not stood aloof from these influences. Some have resisted a little longer than others and some have tried to ignore them. Peploe and Hunter were in their time among the first and most receptive in absorbing fresh impulses.

It is a long time now since the idea was first mooted that the outworn method of grouping works of art into National Schools in galleries and histories should give place to a more enlightened system of comparing artistic procedure and tendencies. It would certainly lead to some fresh assessments, and conceivably it might make it easier to come by a greater knowledge and a richer enjoyment.

It is by comparisons that we arrive at the most competent generalisations, and if as a result we can determine clear national characteristics, so much the better for our patriotism. One may be wrong in thinking it more rewarding to concentrate more on the peculiar personal quality of an artist's communication than on trying to prove that his artistic roots are embedded in his native soil. In due course we shall note the influences which led Peploe, Hunter and Cadell to restore colour to a supremacy in picture-making in a manner that had not been done before in Scotland. They got hints here and there from their immediate past ; gleams from McTaggart, a suggestion from W. Y. Macgregor and perhaps

Arthur Melville, but they found their traditional sources in French Painting.

We can, however, go back further and endeavour to find evidence capable of being defined as conclusive or impressive, which shows any strong national tradition likely to have operated on these three artists or for that matter on any other Scots artist worthy of note.

The Historians

If we turn to the historians Caw and Cursiter, for example, we shall find clear and objective accounts. With all due deference to Cursiter, the approach in W. D. MacKay's book, which he recommends, is not one which appeals to me. Here is a quotation from it :

The ideas propounded in some of the writing of Shaftesbury, and in a treatise concerning Beauty, Order, Harmony and Design by Professor Hutcheson of Glasgow (this treatise is one of the list of volumes Andrew Lumisden, Prince Charles Edward's private secretary, asks his sister to forward to him at Rouen, where he had taken refuge with other Jacobites) had led on, some quarter of a century later, to the works of Winckelmann, Lessing and others, the builders of the Aesthetic philosophy. Aesthetics is a department of knowledge deeply interesting in determining the relation of the Fine Arts to other spheres of mental activity, *but it has always been perilous stuff for the professional artist to meddle with.* [The italics are mine.]

Shades of Leonardo, Blake, Reynolds, Van Gogh, Whistler, Sickert and a host of witnesses ! The same MacKay thought Allan Ramsay mediocre. His attitude to the plastic arts, continued by some successors in the office of Secretary of the Royal Scottish Academy, may help to explain the contrast between the eighteenth and nineteenth centuries in literary Scotland. Why it should be assumed that an artist may neutralise his imagination by the exercise of his intellect seems incomprehensible. Great art is not produced in some kind of trance. An artist who is incapable of thought is incapable of anything but the most transient of emotional impulses.

The Artists

The best instructors in art appreciation in my experience have been practising artists. Peploe was never voluble, but in a short quickly spoken phrase he could be penetrating. Cadell could expatiate at length, and laughter would never be very far away, but from behind the jest an illuminating observation would thrust itself into one's mind. Hunter would disclaim his views with passionate enthusiasm and compel one to share his delight.

It is a great privilege to meet genuine artists. To examine paintings of other artists past and present in their company is an invaluable lesson. How often has one been able to grasp the essence of a picture, to see the main purpose, to read the relevance of every line, every nuance of colour and sense of space through the critical comments of an artist. There are some who only succeed in adding to our confusion. They are, perhaps, only able to be coherent with a paint-brush, but are we right in assuming that theorising is profitless or even dangerous ? Do artists never ' talk shop ' ? We do not require them to become regular teachers but we need them as informed and inspired companions in our fireside books, our studies and in our picture galleries.

Jamesone

It is agreed that native Scottish painters made their appearance in the early seventeenth century, and George Jamesone (*c.* 1587–1644) is usually accepted as the first. He was known as the Scottish Van Dyck, and thus he is described in the title of Bullock's monograph. The Scougalls (there would seem to have been four of them) and their successors in portrait painting derived their inspiration and methods from Dutch or Flemish artists. Similarly, in still-life painting, William Gouw Ferguson, following upon sojourns in Italy and France, finally adopted the style and treatment so brilliantly evolved by the Dutch. His work is of a very high order, as can be seen in the two examples in the Glasgow Art Gallery.

Allan Ramsay

This Continental influence was paramount, and inevitable, since every young Scots artist with high aspirations spent some years in study at one or another of the great European centres of art. Right through the eighteenth century the link with Rome, particularly, is maintained. Allan Ramsay (1713–84), starting at the School of St Luke in Edinburgh, went on to St Martin's Lane Academy in London, where his principal teacher was a Swede, Hans Huyssing, and continued his studies in Rome. But it is generally conceded that his finest work is in the French tradition. At the Exhibition of British Art in Paris some years before the World War II, it was exciting to hear Frenchmen express high opinions on Ramsay. They acclaimed him as a French Painter.

The position held by Ramsay in London was certainly prominent. An interesting account of some of the high lights is given in Stanley Cursiter's *Scottish Art*, but there are some sidelights from Glasgow which are worth recording. In the Hunterian Museum there is a copy of the *Investigator* which contains an essay by Ramsay entitled ' Dialogues on Taste.' There is also a receipt for five shillings from Hogarth to William Hunter for the former's *Analysis of Beauty*. It is said that to anyone buying his prints Hogarth would present a copy of Ramsay's ' Dialogues.' Professor Bryce in *William Hunter and his Museum* has the following : ' Oliver Goldsmith, Allan Ramsay, Dr Burney were among his correspondents, in each case the occasion was some kind of charitable action. Allan Ramsay asks him to see a poor artist and adds, " Being well acquainted with your benevolent disposition I make no apology for the request." ' In Zoffany's picture of a group of Royal Academy members William Hunter is standing next the president, Sir Joshua Reynolds.

There may be great division of opinion as to whether a portrait painter ever produces many works which exist in their own right as great works of art. Here is a piece from Boswell : ' When we got home, and were again at table with

Dr Johnson, we first talked of portraits. He agreed in thinking them valuable in families. I wished to know which he
preferred, fine portraits or those of which the merit was
resemblance.

JOHNSON : Sir, their chief excellence is being like.
BOSWELL : Are you of that opinion as to portraits of ancestors whom
  one has never seen ?
JOHNSON : It then becomes of more consequence that they should
  be like ; and I would have them in the dress of the times which
  makes a piece of history.'

Reynolds has some right to express an opinion. He said :
' The history painter paints man in general. The portrait
painter a particular man—consequently a defective model.'

The Auld Alliance

To return to the point and to acknowledge that Ramsay
is one of Scotland's greatest portrait painters—a modern
rediscovery by the way—he is so not because he was a Scot,
nurtured in a Scottish tradition, but because he was Allan
Ramsay. And if there must be a label it should be ' The
French Tradition.' From this much might be made of the
long-established bonds of friendship between the two countries.
  Shakespeare hints at it :

> But there's a saying, very old and true,—
> If that you will France win,
> Then with Scotland first begin.
>
> *Henry V—Act I, Scene 2*

The pattern of Scotland's cultural history has more than
a few strands which come from France, and these are woven
into a phrase which has a touch of defiance in it—' The Auld
Alliance.' In the field of painting the association alternates
between close and remote, but it has never been broken, and
in the last hundred years it has been closer than ever before.

The Art Schools

Before we pass from the eighteenth century the origin, nature and influence of Art Schools and institutions should be examined. Glasgow can claim the privilege of having had the first art Academy in Scotland. (The St Luke's Academy in Edinburgh never really got going.) It was established by the University printers, Robert and Andrew Foulis, in 1753, antedating the Royal Academy in London by fifteen years. The enterprise was not universally applauded, for Robert Foulis relates, ' There seemed to be a pretty general emulation who should run the scheme down most.' The noble effort failed and the records show that only three of the Foulis Academy students achieved any degree of distinction. These were David Allan, James Tassie and Alexander Runciman. Allan went on to Rome where he remained for eleven years. Tassie became famous for his portrait medallions in wax and made his home in London. Runciman also went to Rome, where a fellow-student, Fuseli, asserted that he was the ' best painter among us.' He returned to Scotland to become the Master of the Edinburgh Trustees' Academy which had been founded in 1760. He developed the teaching methods to make them in line with those practised in Rome. Indeed, the background of teaching and theory at this period was the ' School of Rome.'

Sir Henry Raeburn

Sir Henry Raeburn is commonly described as a self-taught painter—if there is such a thing—but he, too, was in Rome on Reynold's advice for two years. True, he had already established himself as a painter before his journey to Italy, but as an artist he must have had some preferences in what he saw in the work of others. In any event, he does not appear to have inherited any specific Scottish tradition. He may have created one, although it does not appear to have persisted very far into the nineteenth century. Stanley Cursiter with the advantages of his own experience as a portrait painter presents in the course of a fine analysis the following passage which seems to give substance to our argument :

Artists are born, like other people, with a fundamental preference for one set of colours rather than another. It seems to be a peculiarity of the human eye that this colour preference is seldom balanced. One artist may be attracted by red and its complementary green, and another by blues and yellows : still others to whom all colours seem but a tinting of black and white. The artist for whom the whole range of the spectrum is a domain in which he can move without restraint is indeed a rare phenomenon.

Another Scottish portrait painter who, like Ramsay, astonished the London critics when the Scottish Painters exhibition was at Burlington House in 1939 is Andrew Geddes. In his younger days he had a spell in Paris, copying the pictures in the Louvre, but his traditional sources are Rembrandt and Van Dyck as can clearly be noted, especially in his etchings.

Sir David Wilkie

Two observations made by Sir David Wilkie, in addition to giving his point of view as an artist, will help to define the place he occupies in the history of British Art. They are (1) 'I paint, not for those who know, but for those who do not know'; (2) 'To know the taste of the public—to learn what will best please the employers—is to an artist the most valuable of all knowledge.' These must not be lightly dismissed as the cynical comments of an insincere artist. On the contrary, they are the utterances of a 'missionary' confronted by a host of philistines representing a large unsophisticated public without any interest in art. Eventually the artist endeared himself to that public, especially through the medium of engravings made from his most popular paintings, e.g. *The Blind Fiddler*, *The Reading of the Will* and *Blind Man's Buff*.

While it cannot be claimed for Wilkie that he was an

originator of a new form in art, his influence on the art of Victorian England was profound. He popularised the picture which tells a story (defined as *genre* painting) and helped to create a new school of art patron among the middle-classes. The works of the *genre* painters, such as Morland and Wilkie, are really the ancestors of what is still the most popular form of art today, as appearing on our Christmas calendars, the covers of magazines, and as recently exhibited in the Chantrey Bequest exhibition. It is this fact which led the late Roger Fry to say, ' In this respect perhaps Wilkie is more responsible than anyone for much future disaster to our art.' Nevertheless, Fry continues, ' At the same time he was a genuine artist, and was rightly esteemed as such by those who understood that side of his work.'

Teniers and Ostade were his first heroes (Wilkie has been described as ' the Scottish Teniers '), but in his best works he gives an honourable salute to Rembrandt. It is almost entirely on the technical side of his painting that Wilkie has to be linked with the Dutch. Problems of light and shade (chiaroscuro) are handled on traditional lines, but in conception, and frequently in design, there is manifestly an originality which has too often been overlooked.

His first visit abroad was to Paris in 1814. Two years later he was in Holland, but neither of these visits appeared to result in any special change in style. The Dutch painters were well represented in London, and he had already studied them closely. Perhaps he did come back with ideas beyond his capacity, thus leading Ruskin to say, ' Poor Wilkie needs must travel to see the Grand School, and imitate the Grand School, and ruin himself.' Certainly, in his attempt to paint larger-scale pictures of more important subjects he used methods which have not withstood the effects of time. The cracks and wrinkles which have appeared in his later paintings are similar to those which have afflicted the work of many of his contemporaries, notably Raeburn. It is likely that all of them succumbed to the persuasiveness of some artist 'tipster' who had discovered a new method of quick execution, especially for the deep shadows.

In attempting to assess Wilkie's contribution to the development of British Art—and it was an important contribution—it is necessary to take a bird's-eye view of art in Europe at the beginning of the nineteenth century. It has become customary rather to despise the minor painters who had visualised a market for literal and sentimental realism. If their reputations as significant artists have not survived, it is foolish to ignore the fact that they were surpassingly popular in their time. It is equally foolish to fail to examine the reasons for this popularity, and, as has been pointed out, to note that the popular art then established has remained substantially unshaken to this day.

The Domestic Scene

The influence of contemporary literature on the pictorial arts round about 1800 is fascinating on several counts. Wilkie was eleven years old when Robert Burns died, and he lived throughout the period which was enlivened by Sir Walter Scott (1771–1832). The 'domestic painters,' of whom Wilkie was the greatest, had an abundance of material at hand, and even if the actual subjects were not borrowed from the writers of their time, the direction and the treatment were certainly suggested by them. Many works were more or less excellent illustrations, but Wilkie, at his best, created out of his own experience his pictorial theme, which he coloured with his own imagination. As a student he was forced by the formula of the school to devote his time and thought to the classical subject. When he became a free agent he brought something fresh and original into an already established mode and he may have lost some of his greatest qualities when he again took his subject-matter from historical sources. That there is a documentary value in his simple domestic paintings is quite clear, and even if he did stress the story-telling idea of his pictures and sacrificed rather too much to make the point clear, his sense of design nearly always resulted in excellent grouping of his figures. That is to say he could arrange the stage—and he was a very fine draughtsman.

I have dealt with Wilkie at some length for several reasons. The popularity he enjoyed in his lifetime has faded too much and surely he cannot be blamed for the disasters subsequent to his time. The essential artist in him found fuller expression when he latterly changed his theme and treatment. Although this view is contrary to the general trend of opinion, it may be confirmed by comparing two of his works, *The Cottar's Saturday Night* and *Cardinals, Priests and Roman Citizens Washing the Pilgrims' Feet*. They hang near each other in the Glasgow Gallery. And, finally, if it be said of him, as of David Allan, that he translated the Dutch into the Scottish idiom, we must accept it chiefly as it refers to subject-matter and not as an infusion into any well-established painting tradition.

American Opinion

It is sometimes an advantage to see ourselves as others see us. Professor Wallace Notestein in a volume *The Scot in History* which came from the Yale University Press in 1946 has this in a chapter headed 'Decline of the Arts and Rise of Machinery' :

After the death of Sir Henry Raeburn and of Sir David Wilkie there were no painters of distinction, nor any significant school of Scottish painting until the close of the nineteenth century. Within recent time Scottish etchers have become among the best known in the world. As for music, the land which had developed tunes and airs the like of which no other country could claim had, during the larger part of the nineteenth century, little to offer in new airs or in musical composition.

Now we are not compelled to be in absolute agreement with that, but is it so very far from the truth? We have made much of the Rev. John Thomson, the 'father of

Scottish landscape painting,' but he appears to have derived almost everything from Richard Wilson. One of his paintings was sold in London as an early Turner, and too many of his works have become pictorial wrecks. Nevertheless, Thomson opened a door to great possibilities, and the pity of it is that his immediate successors did not build on the foundations he had laid, not in technique but in apprehension.

There is no doubt that the names and works of a number of artists who figure in histories of Scottish Art should be remembered. Some of them have been overrated, and the pick of them with a few exceptions moved to London. The practice of *genre* painting which persisted through the century was performed with greater excellence in the Royal Academy in London. The Scottish practitioners achieved a level little higher than that of the kailyard. They gave us weddings, funerals, massacres, Covenanters, Queens, Kings, schoolmasters, lads and lasses, all with skill, rather less than more, but poles distant from anything worthy to be called significant art. The content was dramatic, religious or sentimental, and they appealed to and moved great numbers of people. Inasmuch as they did that they belong to the history of our Art Academies and Schools, but we are not thereby bound to acclaim these paintings as if they possessed qualities which ought to endure.

Centenaries generally present an occasion for rediscovering the forgotten. Among the most recent is that of David Scott, R.S.A., who is now being reassessed as an imaginative genius. Whose imagination? Not the artist's, for his themes were mainly borrowed. That he designed his pictures with great competence is unquestionable, but his peculiar talent, and it was substantial, was directed to depicting what he knew, not what he felt.

William Dyce (1806–64) is important as an independent in the pre-Raphaelite interlude and J. C. Wintour (1825–82) and Samuel Bough (1822–78), in a reassessment, merit a higher place than is ordinarily given to them.

In the case of Sam Bough, particularly, the knowledge that he started his career as a stage designer has led to the conclusion that his work is primarily theatrical or scenic. Actually he had a very keen eye for whatever was paintable —marine, pastoral or topographical. He could be both tender and vigorous, and his handling of paint gives a hint of things to come. Similarly it was pleasant to hear in 1939 the critics express surprise at the colour quality in Wintour's landscape. It is this 'colour quality' which begins to emerge at the end of the nineteenth century ; it leads us to the main theme and to the idea of a real Scottish Tradition in painting. It also leads us to the fifth in a modest list of great Scots artists : (1) Ramsay, (2) Raeburn, (3) Geddes, (4) Wilkie and (5) McTaggart. The first four are notable in their own rights as artists, but I think William McTaggart (1835–1910) is in addition the real founder of the only tradition likely to grow into a full and recognisable Scottish Tradition.

William McTaggart

McTaggart has been described as ' an original romantic artist, striving always to utter the unutterable, and succeeding in evoking more splendidly than any other Scottish artist the beauty of dancing light and wind and ocean.' That is a very happy and competent definition and comes from Mr John Tonge's little booklet, *The Arts in Scotland.* It was written to coincide with the exhibition of Scottish Art in the Royal Academy, London, in 1939, and I remember it chiefly because of a vigorous discussion among a group of artists, writers and laymen, on What does one mean by an ' original romantic artist ' ? The discussion still goes on, for it appears to be endless. It is difficult to escape from the word. It applies to all the arts, and it seems, in large scale definition, impossible to avoid the labels ' classic ' and ' romantic.' T. S. Eliot says, ' They are a pair of literary terms belonging to literary politics.' We shall try, however, to reach a working hypothesis more precise than the vague idea that 'classic' suggests something with repose and serenity, and 'romantic' something having a sense of restlessness or of disorder. Professor Samuel Alexander puts it thus, 'In the classic the artist goes to meet nature, in the romantic he anticipates nature and imposes himself on the subject.' In other words the romantic outlook is more personal, more subjective, the classical more impersonal, more objective.

An Original Romantic : McTaggart

Now, in claiming McTaggart as an original romantic artist we are also expressing the view that he is the first in Scottish painting. The romantic movement in literature —especially in poetry—goes back to the middle of the eighteenth century. In painting it starts with Constable, although neither he, nor his biographer, Leslie, was aware of it. Although the emergence of romanticism in painting must have been part of a general movement, the significance of Constable's discovery lay in his handling of colour. He made it deeper, richer and used it constructively. By breaking it up into smaller units he gave a vibrating atmospheric quality which was to be exploited in different ways by his successors, particularly in France. It is now well known that his method led Delacroix and, later, the Impressionists, to elevate colour, as did the Venetians, to the supreme place.

Probably we have dramatised too much the independence of McTaggart as a Scottish Impressionist, working quite apart from any French influence though on parallel lines to it. He must have been aware of Turner, who had certainly something to do with the development of Monet, Pissarro and Sisley. If we must have comparison, is there not a more convincing one to be found by placing McTaggart against Wilson Steer (1860–1942)—not because of similarities in their work but as marking developments? Each of them was a modern successor to Constable. Steer's biographer (D. S. McColl) has put on record that the English artist had a respect for the work of McTaggart, although he preferred the smaller pictures. His preference is probably sound, for it seems now that the large impressive canvases which McTaggart often favoured are less effective pictorially than those of small and medium size. When style begins to drift into mannerisms the popular appeal may persist, but the effect of greatness does not endure. It does not seem unreasonable to add that if he had elected to follow the procedure adopted by some of his illustrious predecessors and operated from London, McTaggart's name and work would be more widely known than it is. In any event it was good to see his *Girl Bathing, Kintyre* well placed in the National Collection in Paris immediately before the outbreak of the World War II.

It was Oscar Wilde[1] who said, 'You may have noticed how, for some time, Nature has set herself to resemble the landscapes of Corot.' Whether the sentence was intended to be more than a witticism I do not know, but in the light of experience it has come to have a very special significance. If we believe, as we must believe, that an artist *sees* in nature something not ordinarily perceived by other people (the 'inward meaning' of Wordsworth), and that the impression he receives is expressed in the terms of art, then the natural scene will subsequently recall the artist's impression. That has been my good fortune whenever I have found myself on either the west or east coast of Kintyre. The 'moods' of Kilbrannan Sound as seen from Carradale and the winds of the Atlantic as felt on the shore at Machrihanish always bring to my mind the paintings of William McTaggart. And I am certain that, but for him, I would be missing something. Some day I may be confronted with the work of an unknown artist who has chosen McTaggart's country for his theme. I shall probably then entertain the idea that 'it is not true to nature' to find perhaps (if I still have an open mind) that

[1] Berenson in *Aesthetics and History* (1950) states, ' the witty remark that nature imitates art is justified.' He points out that although attributed to Whistler and Wilde it should be credited to Sainte-Beuve and Goethe and their Greek forerunners.

once again my vision has been widened and my experience enriched. Similarly, Peploe and Cadell, each in his own way, have helped me to sense the imperishable beauty of Iona.

At first, portraiture was McTaggart's main interest, and throughout seven hard years of study he managed to make ends meet by painting portraits during his summer holiday in Ireland. Academic recognition came early to him. He was elected an A.R.S.A. in 1859 and in 1870 was made a full member. (Note the ages—an A.R.S.A. at twenty-four and an R.S.A. at thirty-five, and compare them with the prevailing academic practice today.) His early works, in the tradition of the Scott Lauder School of painting, do not possess any qualities in advance of his important contemporaries, e.g. Pettie and Orchardson. When he began to have confidence in his own creative powers he bothered less with rule-of-thumb methods and adapted himself more and more to what confronted him. This attitude, combined with the change in technique, gives him an important place in the break-away towards a fresh outlook in Scottish painting. That is to say he did not allow rules of training or the recognised masters the right of permanent authority. Consequently he retained the essentials of a proved technique and added what was necessary for the moment. His 'painting philosophy' may be summed up in these hints to a young artist (quoted from Sir James Caw's monograph) :

> The simpler and more direct the method the finer the picture.
>
> Never put a touch on your canvas unless you mean something by it.
>
> There are always accentuated parts in nature and they give life to a picture.
>
> Thick or thin painting does not matter, provided one gets the effect one desires.

The Glasgow School

It has been said that McTaggart influenced the Glasgow School. There is little evidence of this, and it is more likely that Mr Frank Rutter was right when he wrote in his *Modern Masterpieces* : ' What is more than a little remarkable is that, though several of them were acquainted with the work of the French Impressionists, practically none was influenced by the work of McTaggart.'

The Glasgow School (the label was applied by London pressmen as a matter of convenience in describing them) was ' born ' between the years 1880 and 1885. It is generally agreed that the originator was W. Y. Macgregor, who died in 1923, two years after he was made a full R.S.A. Walton, Henry and Paterson were his immediate associates. The group pledged themselves to cut out all the prettiness, sentimentality and anecdote and to give painting its full value and tone, substituting a broad, powerful use of material in place of the niggling, cramped style then in vogue. In 1881 Guthrie, Walton, Henry and Crawhall were working at Brig o' Turk. A year later Guthrie was in Berwickshire, at Cockburnspath, where he was joined by Arthur Melville. They appear to have moved on to Kirkcudbright, where Henry and Hornel joined them. Later, about 1884, Roche and Lavery, returning from Paris, added considerable strength to the movement.

The ' Galloway Landscape '

Many of the recorded opinions of those who at the beginning of the century criticised the Glasgow School contribution I now hold to be no longer valid. Witness what Professor Baldwin Brown has to say on one of the most notable productions of the Glasgow School :

There was at one time, in the nineties of the last century, a theory that the qualities to be aimed at in a picture were those of a Persian carpet, that is to say a colour effect without any effort after demonstrative truth. The heresy was short-lived, but it had its classic expression in the *Galloway Landscape*, which Mr George Henry exhibited at the Royal Scottish Academy in 1891. The moment was one fraught with consequences for the movement, which might easily have been turned in the direction of artistic eccentricity.

Nothing is a stronger proof of the solidity and commonsense which controlled the operations of this somewhat militant minority than the fact that the temptation to scandalise the orthodox was successfully resisted, and the movement went forward on broad and simple lines, with the recognised ideals of all good modern painting held steadily in view.

There can surely be no doubt that if Henry had continued to explore the decorative possibilities of the natural scene instead of troubling himself with ' demonstrative truth,' the Glasgow School as an abiding influence would have extended into this century, and been internationally acclaimed. Many of the younger English artists of today practise the æsthetic doctrines of ' heresy ' exemplified in the Henry picture. Incidentally, the sole survivor of the School, Mr Macaulay Stevenson, thinks the *Galloway Landscape* the finest landscape he has ever seen ' bar Crome's *Mousehold Heath* which is the greatest of all English landscapes.'

' Expressionism '

Notwithstanding the prevailing opinion that its glories have departed, it is to be remembered that, between the Pre-Raphaelites and today, British Art has not known any movement so vital as the Glasgow one. We were reminded of this some years ago by Mr Douglas Percy Bliss (*The Listener*, 1935). It played a great part, following the lead of Whistler, in introducing a fresh concept of the functions of pictorial art. This concept was a phase of the wider movement which originated in Paris and continued to develop there through other phases to the movement of today, to which we may apply the label ' Expressionism.' The argument is that the artist's task is to convey not the objective facts of nature but the subjective feelings of the artist. Sounds like romanticism in a new dress ! The Glasgow School demonstrated this chiefly through a preoccupation with the decorative element in design. Eventually, most of its members appear to have completely lost the early inspiration and their work developed along orthodox or academic lines.

The early traditional influences, which in some cases are very clearly indicated, tended to fade out as the Glasgow School artists developed their own special characteristics. Unlike some contemporary groups, each of them maintained an independent point of view, and the collaboration of the early days did not lead to emotional inbreeding, with resultant feebleness of stock, in the shape of their productions.

Henry, with his departure for the south, seems to have left it to Hornel to maintain the principle that decoration was the chief function of painting. It is often said that Hornel owed much to the Japanese and to Monticelli. His debt to the former is clear, but I find it difficult to see any strong connecting link between him and the latter. They shared a fondness for juicy colour, but each used it differently, utilising it generously for new and personal ends. Hornel reached a stage when fresh adventures and experiments no longer appealed to him, but he stands as one of the two most original members of the School. The other is, in my considered opinion, Stuart Park. (I know this opinion may produce gasps of astonishment.) Stuart Park was not in the inner circle of the movement and his range of pictorial interests is limited. Early essays in portraiture promised great results, but he switched over to flowers with ' decoration' as his motto. One stroke of the brush = one petal. There was nothing new in this, for Sargent had done the same thing for Eton collars in his schoolboy portraits. But Park had an unusual sense of colour which was very much his own. He makes white appear colourful in a way that is certainly unique, and the little tricks which disturb the technicians are to me nothing more than the recognisable handwriting of a man who wants to tell us something—not everything—about flowers. Stuart Park might be described as a semi-abstractionist. I had one of his paintings hanging between two works by Raoul Dufy, a modern ' eccentric ' and a most powerful colourist, and they all seemed very happy together.

Walton and Roche have gone up and down in public favour. Their pictures suffer greatly in black-and-white reproduction because the colour contrast and tonal values generally are of a subtle order. In front of the actual pictures one is led to think, 'Here are the poets of the School.' Walton derived his inspiration from Constable and Corot, but in his characteristic landscapes he is a lyricist who is confident of his own powers, even if he is over-anxious not to strike a wrong note. Roche seems to take more interest in how he says it than in what he says.

Joseph Crawhall was remarkable in a variety of ways. He stands by himself in that he is substantially uninfluenced by any school of painters, and he has not begotten any successors worthy of comparison. His animal sketches are little masterpieces, but his more notable works such as *The Spangled Cock* are so brilliantly executed and so meticulously complete that they almost drift out of the realm of art.

Arthur Melville, in the water-colour medium, was undoubtedly a creative artist. He pointed a way along which many have followed, not only by making use of his technical experiments but also by borrowing freely his ideas in design. It will be noted later that Melville had something to do with Cadell's early essays.

Scottish Art Review

The general cultural activity of the Glasgow School period was reflected in a kind of way by the appearance of the *Scottish Art Review* in 1888. The story of its origin must await another occasion. But I think the aim and purpose of this publication is worth quoting. It was: 'To further a knowledge and a love of that aspect of divine truth which it is the privilege of art to present to men—a knowledge and a love which this nation stands in dire need of at the present day.' This is as fitting today as it was in 1888.

Well, the Glasgow School petered out as a movement, although it did for a time put Scotland on the art map of

Europe. Macaulay Stevenson gave me some advice when I once proposed giving a talk on the subject. ' Ca' canny in ascribing something phenomenal to our " boys." There were some good artists among them and they helped in bringing painting back to its own language instead of bending it to literature and history.'

So we turn again to individuals, and in the Glasgow School we find W. Y. Macgregor and Arthur Melville supplying the continuity which is essential to any tradition. Peploe, Hunter and Cadell—particularly Cadell—are in the line, but France rather than Scotland exercises the greater influence.

The history of the Glasgow School requires to be re-written. In the early days the work was very strongly derivative, but the particular influences were transient in their effect. The link with the New English Art Club and the part generally played by the Glasgow artists within the gamut of British Art has not yet received the attention the movement merited. And the common error that it was a school of artists working in the same manner falls to be corrected. They were united in earnestness and determination but they were individualists. Each of them had his bias towards tendencies which were manifest in their elders or contemporaries in France or Holland. Whistler was a hero, and it was due to the energy and persistence of the young Glasgow artists that the city acquired the famous Carlyle portrait in the face of considerable opposition. (This was in 1891, some months before *The Mother* was purchased for the Luxembourg.) Some of the Glasgow ' boys ' became absorbed with tone and pattern (supposed features of the Scottish tradition), others with the play of light, but the sources of any originality were on the Continent, and if they could not go there the dealers and collectors in Glasgow had the pictures which could be studied in comfort. There was also the civic Collection, and it may be of interest to note how much the tiny bit of landscape in the Giorgione at Kelvingrove may have directed the minds of some of the group back to the Venetian School of painting and helped to augment the increased concern with colour as the chief end in painting.

THREE SCOTTISH COLOURISTS

The roots of any contemporary British artist to whom it is competent to apply the description ' colourist ' are to be found in the English artist John Constable.   His importance has long been recognised, and in recent years this has been most emphatically demonstrated in the high prices his works command in the auction room.   Scholars and historians are also expanding in contemporary literature the space devoted to the consideration of Constable's special influence on European painting.   Sir Charles Holmes in his introduction to the Everyman Library edition of Leslie's biography of Constable observed that the artist's work is a record ' of the most momentous aesthetic revolution which Europe has experienced for at least three centuries.'   He also says, oddly enough, that the claim that ' Constable is generally held to be the father of modern landscape both in France and England ' must not be pressed too far ;   presumably because French painters in general would have had nothing but the memory of the few works by Constable exhibited in the Paris Salon.   ' It is as a tradition rather than a reality that his influence has persisted ' we are told.   This seems incomprehensible, and it is certainly not based on facts or on any degree of likelihood.   Tradition, in the absence of direct contact with the works on which it is supposed to rest, cannot, it seems to us, exercise an influence of real significance. Actually, twenty-seven paintings by Constable were purchased by French collectors, chiefly through the dealer Arrowsmith. Later, in 1874, Van Gogh writes to his brother Theo with enthusiasm over the Constables he had seen in London and how they reminded him of Diaz and Daubigny !   And through direct questioning I have been informed that Constable's work has been studied in France as a routine in teaching.   Moreover, Constable himself was not influenced by what he saw in public galleries or exhibitions, but by what he saw in private collections, notably that of Sir George Beaumont. It was there he paid homage to Claude and Rubens, for he never set foot out of England.

Development through France

It is not possible here to trace the development of painting through France in the nineteenth century, nor to examine how the great artists adapted the old or invented the new technical methods in the handling of paint. The changes which take place on a national scale can often be seen in miniature when one attempts to mark the stages in an individual artist's growth.

Take Peploe, for instance. In his early work the salute to Franz Hals is apparent. Then in turn come Chardin, Manet, Pissarro and Cézanne, each of them contributing something either in the matter of technique or by initiating a fresh conception concerning the meaning and purpose of art. Out of it all eventually comes the personal element which makes the whole lifetime of production worthy to be remembered and honoured. So with Hunter and Cadell, each with his different background, with his imitative periods and then emerging into the realm of personal achievement. What, if anything, makes them a little greater than most of their contemporaries? Berenson says that no-one has yet painted the perfect landscape, because thus far ' only a few aspects have been expressed, but not all.' Is it because these three, among others, have, in addition to an equal command of the means to express colour, supplied a revelation that is not a constant feature in the thousands of canvases which decorate the walls of recurrent exhibitions? That perhaps remains to be seen.

J. D. Fergusson

Early in this century Glasgow and Edinburgh were good places for artists. The newcomer certainly had his trials and tribulations, but he stood a fair chance of achieving some degree of recognition. In the West the Glasgow School had stirred the artistic world out of its complacency, and the Royal Institute of Fine Arts, chiefly through intelligent and courageous borrowing of important works, made its annual exhibition a notable art event. J. D. Fergusson, an Edinburgh man, says that in his young days Glasgow was the centre, because between the usual art exhibitions and the dealers there always seemed to be more general activity, more enlightened talk and more alluring prospects.

Fergusson's association with the new spirit of the time, and particularly with the artists under discussion, is of course an intimate one. Indeed, he is one of ' Les Peintres Ecossais ' as they became known in Paris. Unlike the others, he made his home more or less permanently in Paris, returning to Scotland in 1939 to encourage earnest and sincere young artists of this generation.[1] His life-long friendship with Peploe will be noted later, but his part in the struggle to find a responsive public must not be overlooked. It is also fitting to place on record that Peploe, Hunter and Cadell owed much of the success they achieved in their lifetime to the practical support and encouragement of art dealers in Glasgow, Edinburgh and elsewhere.

Alexander Reid

Alexander Reid, the Glasgow art dealer had an international reputation. As a young man he was sent to Paris to gain a wider experience in one of the famous firms in that city. He worked with Boussod & Valadon (successors to Goupils) and one of his associates was Theo, brother of Vincent Van Gogh. For a period he shared rooms with the artist who was to become famous, but the eccentricities rather than the artistic genius of his room-mate appear to have made the greater impression. The association, however, is happily recalled through the survival of an excellent portrait of Reid by Van Gogh. Contacts were also made with

---

[1] Glasgow University conferred on him the degree of LL.D. in 1950

all the leading figures in the Paris world of art, and it is not surprising to know that when he eventually started out in business for himself he tried to introduce French paintings into Scotland.

The civic records show that Alexander Reid must have organised a completely new firm in 1891. From 1886–91 there is in the directory no entry of Kay and Reid, his father's firm. The new firm assumed the high-sounding title of ' Société des Beaux-Arts ' with a gallery at 232 West George Street. It continued in business at various addresses until 1926 when an amalgamation with a London firm took place. The Glasgow end of the business was given up in 1931, and the direct successor to the Reid firm is now the Lefevre Gallery in London.

When Reid started in business the Glasgow School was just beginning to emerge. He was on intimate terms with nearly every member of the group and organised exhibitions not only in Glasgow but also in London and Germany. Some of the exhibitions were successful, some were not, but for a long time his gallery was the centre of activity.

Although his chief interest, for financial reasons, was directed towards pushing the sale of important works by well-known artists, Reid was responsible for introducing younger men of promise to old and new patrons. And Reid's verdict carried authenticity. He bought and sold McTaggart paintings with an enthusiasm which tended to make prices soar beyond a true market value. But the excitement of the ' boom ' period and of record auction prices was matched by his delight in giving a young artist his first ' one-man ' show.

Aitken Dott

Peploe, the Edinburgh artist, had his first dealer's exhibition in Aitken Dott's in 1909. His first Glasgow exhibition was in Reid's in 1915 although it is certain that a few pictures were included in mixed exhibitions before that date. Some slight and tentative efforts by Peploe had been exhibited in the Glasgow Institute as early as 1896. Exhibitions alternated generally between Aitken Dott's and Reid's. The odd occasions in London, Paris and New York were usually arranged through the influence of the Glasgow firm.

Cadell operated more independently, relying on group exhibitions and direct sales. Of course he too had his ' one-man ' shows, but he does not appear to have been so closely linked with the two firms, Aitken Dott in Edinburgh and Reid in Glasgow, as were Peploe and Hunter.

In his book on Peploe, Stanley Cursiter pays tribute to Mr P. McOmish Dott, the principal of the Aitken Dott firm. He was a man ' of fine taste, generous and warm-hearted and a real friend to many of the artists he encouraged and supported.' I was not privileged to know him, but I became well acquainted with Mr George Proudfoot who continued the firm's interest in the work of Peploe, Hunter and Cadell, an interest which is still maintained by his family.

The two firms for many years shared in ' campaigning ' for the younger Scottish artists who had something fresh to say. This was often done before they were given a ' hearing ' on the walls of the art institutions.

In the matter of finding purchasers for their works Peploe and Hunter were alike. They acted upon the assumption that painting a picture and selling a picture were two distinct jobs. The latter should be left to those who knew the technique of salesmanship, whatever that may mean. In the days preceding and leading into the 1914 War it meant something. In the case of Peploe, particularly, it brought Duncan Macdonald on the scene.

Duncan Macdonald and A. J. McNeill Reid

Duncan Macdonald started his illustrious career as an art dealer in Glasgow. When in 1914 war broke out, he was, much to his disgust and disappointment, found to be medically incapacitated from army service. Adapting himself to circumstance he moved to Edinburgh and subsequently joined the Aitken Dott firm under George Proudfoot. At first, his interest and energies were centred on the graphic arts and he acquired high authority on etchings and etchers. Very soon, however, he graduated into colour and was responsible for making known to a number of people, including myself, the importance of Peploe in the field of contemporary Scottish painting. He joined A. J. McNeill Reid in 1926 and moved to London, eventually winning for himself a high place in international art-dealing circles. He died in 1949.

McNeill Reid entered his father's business in 1913. Reid senior had maintained his Paris contacts and the McNeill in his son's name indicates a close friendship with Whistler who was a godfather. The firm, in addition to 'importing' the works of well-known French painters of the nineteenth century continued to keep abreast of the times by exhibiting the so-called ' moderns.'

Notwithstanding the inevitable widening of influences and interest, Reid and Macdonald still retained the early high opinion of the value and importance of the Scottish colourists in the field of British painting. It was Macdonald who took the leading part in organising the exhibition of Les Peintres Ecossais in Paris in 1931. For ten years (1929–1939) I was one of his business associates along with McNeill Reid, and it may be said of each of us that we maintained contacts with Glasgow and Edinburgh, and with Peploe and Hunter, in spite of the attractions and excitements of picture-dealing in London, Paris and New York. Cadell was more elusive in that he isolated himself so much in Iona that meetings with him were much less frequent.

The Royal Scottish Academy and The Glasgow Institute

It was chiefly through the dealers that the works of Peploe, Hunter and Cadell were brought to the notice of a discerning public. But, as always, there is more than one factor concerned. The Royal Scottish Academy and the

Glasgow Institute in due course accepted the ' moderns ' and not necessarily because they had begun to conform to official standards. It was more likely because of the increasing pressure of enlightened opinion. Probably the advantages of including some works which, in spite of their ' crudity,' did convey a sense of vitality and originality, appealed to the respective councils. There is nothing unique in the records of rejections, which was the experience of all three ; it is a common experience. Cadell, as far as can be discovered, was alone in submitting work to the Royal Academy in London. Peploe and he subsequently became members of the Royal Scottish Academy, but Hunter, chiefly through lack of interest, had no academic aspirations.

Obviously no artist can expect to achieve a worth-while career in his profession if the public display of his work is limited to a picture or two in annual exhibitions. The chief elements in the necessary propaganda are (a) ' one-man ' shows, (b) group exhibitions, (c) the enthusiasm of patrons, (d) press notices, criticism and appreciative articles on their individual contributions or on the special art activity of kindred workers.

Criticism : Publicity

The various exhibitions and the warm-hearted support of collectors in Scotland, and their bearing on their lives and work are noted elsewhere, but it is perhaps of value to remember how they fared at the hands of critics and publicists. Peploe, the eldest, was not cordially acclaimed in Sir James Caw's *Scottish Painting* (1908). He was then thirty-seven years old and had been exhibiting in public for about ten years. ' His [Peploe's] vision is not very subtle, and he is possessed by a perverse taste for the ugly or the bizarre in figure and landscape . . . some of his landscapes too, cleverly though they are placed upon the canvas and admirably as they sometimes record flashing effects of light are too reminiscent of such masters as Sisley and Pissarro to be quite convincing.' In that same year *Head of a Woman* which was exhibited in London was greeted by the critics as a great achievement. The situation now appears to be reversed. In fairness to Sir James Caw, it must be said that he was not antagonistic to young artists. He knew the difficulties and uncertainties, the attempts and failures, of the searcher after new ways of stating old truths. His opinion was common currency, and it was then exceptional to find in Scotland any writer willing to acknowledge that something new and important was happening. There were two—John Ressich who fought hard, with great sympathy and intelligence, both by using his pen and by urging his influential friends to buy, and Blackie Murdoch who, in 1910, included an appreciation of Peploe in a volume of essays.

London and Paris

Later on when the attempt to test opinion in the south was made, the late Frank Rutter and Charles Marriott, for many years Art critic to *The Times*, welcomed in various publications, in qualified terms it is true, the new Scottish group. Throughout the ensuing years, however, it was J. D. Fergusson who had the best ' press.' He was better known, for he exhibited with more regularity in Paris and London. ' Scotland is a long way off, even by train,' observes a critic in *The Listener* (April 1949). He goes on to administer a hefty rebuke, under the guise of a review of ' Scottish Art ' by Stanley Cursiter, for our inability to distinguish provincialism from patriotism.

They appear to have been better informed or more concerned in Paris. Peploe, Hunter and Cadell, in the two exhibitions held there, were welcomed as Scottish artists with a specific national quality, and the French Government acquired two works by Peploe and one by Hunter.

By and large all three, in their lifetime, failed to command any substantial degree of recognition in London. In the Exhibition of Scottish Art at Burlington House in 1934 the small architectural room was given to ' examples of the " more advanced " and emphatic phases of recent paintings in Scotland,' to quote the catalogue. In it were twenty-one Peploes, eight Cadells, five Hunters, along with two by Walter Grieve, and one each by W. Y. Macgregor, Corsan Morton and William Crozier. Apart from reflecting the views of the organisers, this section of the exhibition received an undue amount of attention relative to the whole display. Peploe, Hunter and Cadell were selected for most of the critical comments, of which this is one : ' Peploe in particular was an excellent painter, but there is a feeling that these recent Scottish artists did not know quite what to do about colour as between its constructive and its decorative function.' Now, as I understand it, and to state it briefly, the ' constructive function ' means that use of colour by which an artist ' places ' the component parts of his picture. Certain colours will bring forward or push back passages in the painting. Cézanne, who rediscovered the constructive use of colour, could place a tree, house or mountain exactly where he wanted it. The Glasgow School were certainly more concerned with the decorative function of colour, but the three Scottish colourists, following the lead from France, began to use colour constructively. Peploe and Hunter were not the first perhaps, but they were among the first in Britain to understand what Cézanne was attempting to do, and they never ceased to be aware of colour as the fundamental element in pictorial art and that its constructive function was all-important. Cadell follows more closely in the direct line through W. Y. Macgregor.

Originality and Plagiarism

It seems to some, however, that we are in danger of exaggerating the original or creative contribution made by these artists to Scottish painting, that they are indeed little more than competent eclectics. Arguing on the hypothesis that the greatest art is that which gives the greatest pleasure to the greatest number of normal human beings over the greatest length of time, the discussion might well be left to posterity. But because British Art of the present generation may eventually acquire the description ' the eclectic phase ' the matter is worth a little consideration.

If we are looking for evidences of plagiarism in works of art the search will become endless. Nature is everybody's property and all art consists in giving new forms to old ideas. At first these forms are borrowed, and if effective use is made of them reputations are established because the artist has not deviated from the traditionalism which is easily understood and appreciated. In witness of this is Peploe's experience with McOmish Dott, who deplored the change in style when Peploe had struck out on new and original lines. Similarly with Hunter and Cadell who had to resist appeals to return to their earlier methods. Style in painting is formed in two ways, first by a study of pictures and second by the observation of Nature. If the latter is inadequately performed we continue to receive the familiar ' in the manner of ' production. From personal knowledge I can vouch that all three artists in the full exercise of their talents turned to the prime source of inspiration—Nature. If this is not discernible in their work may it not be that the critic with the funded experience derived from a knowledge of past and present ' Schools ' is unable to measure the personal equation ? As in literature, so in art ; when we start out on the journey towards distinction we are all pathetic little plagiarists. It is given to the few to emerge into the light of new pathways, and limiting the claim to Scottish Art that is what happened to these—Peploe, Hunter and Cadell.

True originality in painting is development. An artist either imitates technique or adapts it to suit himself. In the matter of subject there are no exclusive rights. These three artists did not indulge in the cult of minor art. They recognised the giants and they refused to produce for the entertainment of tired minds. When an artist edges away

44

from his traditional background into a fresh adventure he may become an artist who matters—not necessarily great because he may not possess enough of the qualities which make for greatness. But he will have risen above the common level and become entitled to serious consideration.

Classicism and Romanticism

When we turn to another critical comment (see page 12), to the effect that Peploe because of his facility reduced Cézanne's style to a formula, we can rely on factual evidence. Peploe was tormented by every problem in painting. His family was constantly aware of the strain. Nothing came to him easily, either in conception or execution. There was a strong bond of affinity between him and Cézanne, whom he acknowledged as his master, and it is this. Cézanne threw his ' failures ' out of the window. When Peploe was exasperated by his ' failures ' he turned the canvas and started afresh on the other side. Perhaps that is in the tradition of the canny Scot !

It is probably impossible for anyone to know whether the effect of a work of art upon the spectator is ever precisely what the artist had in mind when he responded to the urge to express himself. Nevertheless a partial or imperfect result is not quite the same thing as a complete failure. To each his preference, and to the critic or historian the right to assess and to record values in time and place. If we must make distinctions and classifications it is not far off the mark to describe Peploe as the Classicist, Hunter as the Romanticist and Cadell as somewhere between the two.

In Peploe's work we are aware of an artist who is compelled by something inherent in the theme and who seeks to give it rational expression in paint. Hunter under similar compulsion cares less about the means and sustains the emotional reaction through to the finished work. Maybe this is why he was less successful when he took the matter beyond the range of feeling. Cadell alternated between the calculated, orderly and organised project and the daring quick attack to capture the fleeting impression.

Dr A. C. Barnes in discussing the elements of painting in *The Art in Painting* concludes the section on colour with this sentence, ' That colour-relations are all-important in plastic form, that composition at its best is effected by means of colour, is one of the most weighty facts in aesthetics, and it is one to which the great majority of writers on plastic art seem to be totally oblivious.'

The preparation of this book is a measure of our agreement, and it does not matter so very much to us if the Scots to whom we pay tribute fail to become well known outwith the national boundaries. They have given and continue to give delight to thousands and, who knows, they may have blazed a trail for a noble band of successors.

S. J. Peploe
1871–1935

S. J. Peploe with Willy and Denis at Cassis, 1924

S. J. Peploe

1871–1935

SAMUEL JOHN PEPLOE was born in Edinburgh on the 27th January 1871. His father, Robert Luff Peploe, had a distinguished career as a banker, eventually reaching the highest executive post, general manager, in the Commercial Bank of Scotland. His mother, Anne Watson, came from Campbeltown, where her father was the agent for the same bank. Her grandfather was a provost of the burgh and had some association with Liverpool and the shipping industry. On his father's side Peploe's ancestry has been traced to Shropshire, and various interesting conjectures have been made on the origin of the family name, but from 1800 the family tree has had its roots in Scotland.

Peploe was three years old when his mother died and twelve when his father died. Along with an elder brother and younger sister his early life was controlled by executors, who did their utmost to counter an early ambition towards art as a career. Following school-days at the Collegiate School in Charlotte Square, Peploe attended Edinburgh University, but did not graduate. His eldest brother, James, was destined for the Army and seldom, if ever, showed any interest in the arts. The Services and sport became his chief preoccupations, and his four sons—one in the Army and three in the Navy—continued the tradition. James died a few days before his brother, S. J. Peploe.

Another brother, Willie to all his friends, was placed in his father's bank. He had shown an early bent towards painting and was the possessor of considerable talent. S. J. in his turn was directed to Law, but the view from the office

49

window had more attractions than the deeds on the desk, and once outside the office he found it much too easy to forget to return. Law, therefore, had to be ruled out, but the adventure was abandoned without ill-feeling. Indeed Peploe in an autobiographical moment with J. D. Fergusson, recalled the final interview with the head of the firm thus, ' So, young man, you prefer the beauty of Princes Street Gardens and Art to the austerity of this office and the law. Are you sure you have the divine afflatus ? You know, it is often confused with wind in the stomach.'

The colonies, the Army and the Church were each given consideration, but in the end authority surrendered and art won the day. Peploe attended the Edinburgh School of Art and later studied in Paris at Julien's and elsewhere. Evidently he conformed to the rules of student-days for he achieved the distinction of medal awards on at least two occasions. In Paris he enjoyed the companionship of Robert Brough, a brilliant young fellow-student, whose tragic death in a railway accident in 1905 was a severe loss to the younger generation in the then contemporary movement in Scottish Art.

When he returned to Scotland, Peploe discovered that the finest restorative after a period of over-concentration on work was somewhere in the outer Hebrides. Accompanied by his brother Willie or R. C. Robertson he would generally end up on the island of Barra. Arriving tired and jaded, in a day or two he would become full of vigour and eager to paint. The two Peploes and Robertson, each in his own way, ' tackled ' Barra in sketch-book or on canvas with enthusiasm. S. J., with a fuller equipment in the way of training and with his keener perception, extracted more of the essential qualities, as is evidenced in the small panels which have survived. While these give the merest hint of changes in the use of colour, the ' calligraphy ' which makes the signature ' Peploe ' so unnecessary in the later paintings is easily identified.

When in a reminiscent mood, S. J. and his brother would recall some of the holiday experiences and retell them with great relish. They once took the ' long route ' to the Isles, from Oban, by Skye and Uist, to Castlebay. It was June and the weather was calm. The sea and islands seemed unreal and so very lovely that they sat on deck all night. When the ship, the *Staffa*, reached Dunvegan in the afternoon there was, as usual, a big crowd on the pier to meet the steamer—the one event and excitement of the day. On this particular afternoon the crowd was behaving in a very extraordinary manner. Some were slapping their faces, their arms and legs, others were waving handkerchiefs, and all of them were stamping or jumping around with great activity. As the *Staffa* crept closer to the pier, the cause of the commotion became abundantly clear. It was a swarm of midges, and very soon the dance on the pier was equalled in zeal by the dance on the deck. Peploe always asserted that the Skye midge is the most persistent, most elusive and most irritating of all insects, and he had no difficulty in accepting the legend that the Highland Fling was first danced on the pier at Dunvegan.

In the midst of these enjoyable excursions to the Western Isles, Peploe was constantly engaged in perfecting his art. He early recognised that drawing was the essence of any well-organised picture and he was never without a sketch-book. It has been said that he was a born draughtsman, and there is no doubt that he possessed unusual gifts ; but he always kept ' trying out ' different methods in treatment, thereby evolving a style which became more personal with the passing of the years. Peploe never ceased to be aware of the fact that while a craftsman need not become an artist, an artist must also be a craftsman. He was, of course, conversant with the fine pictures in the National Gallery and saw in the annual exhibitions of the Royal Scottish Academy those loaned works by contemporary continental painters which were generally included. A visit to Holland brought him into direct contact with a fuller range of work by the Dutch Masters, and in one or two of his early portraits the Franz Hals influence is certainly discernible. It is customary to make a list of the great continental painters who are supposed to have contributed to Peploe's various periods and styles, Chardin, Manet, Cézanne, etc. ; but it is equally important to recognise that the significant values in any young artist's painting, that is, the pictorial values, are also shaped by all the competent artists of his own time. And this fact should save us from indulging too much in extravagant partisan claims on behalf of any individual.

At the very first exhibition to which Peploe contributed in the early nineties, his three small oil paintings—two landscapes and a head—were hung beside McTaggart, Roche, Hornel and other Scottish painters, especially those of the Glasgow School. The head was a salute to Whistler, a salute which the Glasgow School had made some years earlier. Indeed, it is more than probable that the general activity and the sustained concentration on treatment, as distinct from theme, which marked the closing years of the nineteenth century were the outstanding factors in Peploe's development. Clearly he was constantly on the search, always learning, and if he felt moved to ' test ' a new line of approach, not even the advantages of a sure and certain patronage would hold him back. This attitude is important, for more than once in his career Peploe resisted all efforts to persuade him to conform to the Wilkie rule. (See page 21.)

That he elected to make his home permanently in Scotland, when evidence of a larger and more understanding public in the south was unmistakable, cannot have been altogether a domestic matter. The art atmosphere in Edinburgh may have had its periods of stuffiness, but an odd breeze would blow up from the west, and on the whole it may be said that an artist can and should help to create the appropriate environment for his art as well as for his way of life. He never became obsessed with any idea or theory, and it is proper to emphasise that from the outset he recognised one important essential—that since the result of any emotion

Plate I

ROSES AND FRUIT ON TABLE   Oil $6\frac{1}{2} \times 9\frac{1}{2}$ in.

must be expressed in concrete form, the very nature of art presupposes the knowledge and practice of the technique of painting. An artist must certainly be free to follow his own fancy, but he has also to be interested in visual facts and in the formal laws of painting. What he may have gained from the Art Schools is difficult to determine—he called Bouguereau of Julien's a damned old fool—what he gained from direct study of the Dutch and French Masters and from contact with his alert contemporaries is more certain. And the interests and talks were not limited to painting.

J. D. Fergusson, a lifelong friend, has retained very happy memories of their early associations in France and Scotland. He has put on record how much they were impressed by what they saw in the visits to the Luxembourg and to Durand-Ruel (the famous French dealer who championed the Impressionists). Peploe, according to J. D., had steeped himself in George Moore's *Modern Painters* and Zola's *L'Œuvre*, and was familiar with the writings of Walter Pater, Arthur Symons, Henry James, Wilde and Meredith. They discussed the accepted and tentative theories, and on one occasion spent an afternoon on the rocks at the northern tip of Islay reading Pater's essay on the ' Mona Lisa.' They were also interested in music, especially in the work of the young composers in France, because they felt there was some relationship between ' modern ' music and ' modern ' painting. One of J. D.'s happiest memories is that of S. J. playing on an old Dettmar piano in the former's Paris studio.

For several years they spent happy painting holidays together at Etaples, Paris-Plage, Dunkirk, Berneval, Dieppe, Etretat, Le Tréport and other French seaport towns or villages. They worked all day, drawing or painting, and thoroughly enjoyed the French food and wine. ' I mean good food,' said J. D. when telling me of those happy days, ' not fantastic food ; good peasant food in France, good Scots food in Scotland, and we took time to it—time to eat and talk and draw all the things on the table.' J. D. also added this :

I remember when we arrived at Dunkirk. I laughed at the lightness of the railway carriages and S.J. said, ' What's the matter with them, aren't they adequate ? ' That was characteristic of him. In his painting and in everything he did he tried to make things adequate ; his satisfaction was a severe synthesis ; to find, by persistent trial, the essentials. He worked all the time from Nature but never imitated it. He often took a long time to make contact with a place and was discouraged by a failure. He wanted to be sure of a thing before he started and seemed to believe that you could be sure. I don't think he wanted to have a struggle on the canvas ; he wanted to be sure and that gave his painting something.

This approach was not a constant feature in Peploe's method. If it were, it would have placed an undue emphasis on the craftsmanship side of his painting. If an artist works out everything in his mind and then starts out to express it without further qualification, he may be a very good painter but he is not likely to be a very good artist.

J. D. stayed on in Paris but Peploe remained faithful to Edinburgh. At various studios—Shandwick Place, Devon Place and York Place—he continued to produce pictures. Cursiter seems to indicate that his first one-man show at Aitken Dott's was in 1909. Actually it was some years earlier—in 1903. The records show that twelve paintings were sold, one of them to J. D. Fergusson for £15. (See Plate 2.) At the 1909 exhibition Peploe had forty-eight drawings and sixty-three paintings comprising still-lifes, flowers, figures and landscapes, a retrospective survey of his formative years. His first exhibited work appeared in the Glasgow Institute in 1896. The Society of Scottish Artists gave him a place in the following year, but it was not until 1901 that his name appears in the catalogue of the Royal Scottish Academy. The fact that the R.S.A. rejected his work more than once did not appear to disturb Peploe or create in him any feelings of frustration or exasperation. He paid little heed to some of his contemporaries who, smarting under similar experiences, advised him to ignore the annual exhibitions, for he continued to send regularly to the Glasgow Institute and the R.S.A. throughout the subsequent years. But he never painted specially for these exhibitions nor had them in mind when planning his work. He selected from available canvases those he thought might be acceptable and left it at that.

This 1909 exhibition must have given the art-interested public the first chance to see what might be the significant trends in Scots painting arising in the new century and coming out of the Glasgow School experiment in the old. Probably Sir James Caw's criticism, already noted, was also directed towards the evidence of a too close affinity with the Impressionists. There is no doubt that, in the pictures painted at Comrie, Manet has given place to Monet. There is even a hint that he may have been aware of Vuillard— the Vuillard of the early nineties. Peploe's visits to Comrie were due to the fact that his sister had married Dr Frederick Porter who was engaged there in medical practice. Dr Porter was very much interested in painting and was possessed of a sufficient talent to justify public exhibition of his work in very good company. His account of Peploe at work is worth recording.

One day I watched him painting outside the gateway of my house. It was a brilliant afternoon and Peploe was painting a 24 × 20 canvas, embracing a roadway of Dalginross with some whitewashed cottages, and with a background of low-lying hill. In the immediate foreground, to the left of the canvas, there was a woman with a dark sunshade. Beyond this and more centrally placed was a horse and cart. I watched Peploe while he was painting the figure and the horse and cart, and it was a revelation to me with what dexterity and precision those moving objects took their place in the picture. It was in such cases that his masterly draughtsmanship was revealed ; with a few strokes of his brush those objects became living things. Another day I watched him at work ; it was a luminous grey day, and he was painting a small canvas near the banks of the river Earn. In the composition there was a tree with a tortuous trunk on the left of the canvas. He had a difficulty in getting the proper curve of the tree to carry out the rhythm of the picture. With a rapid sweep of

55

his brush he drew the curve, but it was not right. Again he tried, and I remember that six attempts were made before he was satisfied. For here, as in all his pictures, the final result must show no ambiguity. It had to be accomplished without any signs of hesitancy or weakness in the technique. Every stroke must have a meaning to express what it was intended to express.

Even before 1909, and certainly from then on, patrons were found through the art dealers. Reid appears to have been the first to appreciate that a new young Scots artist with something original to say had arrived. He had noticed Peploe's work when the artist was quite young and had continued to buy odd pictures, with which he would persuade his customers to be on the outlook for more. The Aitken Dott firm in Edinburgh also gave Peploe a prominent place on their list of promising young artists, and the collaboration between the Glasgow and Edinburgh firms continued, with minor variations, for many years. Each of them merits acknowledgment for the recognition and encouragement given to the young Scots artist at a time when a lack of both might have had a very damaging effect.

I have heard it said that Peploe ' burned himself out ' before 1910. The absurdity of the observation becomes apparent in an inspection of his subsequent paintings and in the nature of his different phases. It is much more relevant and nearer the mark to say that the real Peploe, the independent, creative artist began to blossom about this time.

The year 1910 was notable for three reasons. Chief among these was his marriage to Miss Margaret Mackay, for there was then created the ideal companionship which profoundly influenced and sustained Peploe throughout the remainder of his life. It was also the beginning of a period of residence in France where art was undergoing a series of experimental essays, with effects which were to produce alarm, not to say consternation, throughout the world. And in November of that same year Roger Fry took the lead in

MHOR, MULL, FROM IONA   Oil 20 × 28 in.

Plate III

ROSES AND STILL LIFE   Oil 29 × 20 in.

organising the first Post-impressionist exhibition in the Grafton Galleries in London.

In Paris the Peploes took a studio in the Boulevard Raspail. It was bright and gay, the decoration having been completed by S. J. himself in accordance with his newly formed ideas on colour, ideas which he began to express with an increased intensity in his painting. Life for both of them was full and varied. They loved Paris with its easy pleasant café life, where they met their friends at noon and at seven in the evening. It was usually the same restaurant, Boudet's, where they were mothered by Augustine, a wonderful woman from the Côte-d'Or. After dinner they would go on to another favourite haunt for coffee and music with J. D. Fergusson, Anne Rice the American painter, Jo Davidson the sculptor, Roffy the poet and La Torrie, mathematician and aviator. E. A. Taylor and Jessie King were often in their company, forming another Scottish link, and on occasion Michael Sadler, Middleton Murry and Katherine Mansfield would join them. The names alone are a sufficient indication of the nature, quality and range of the discussions. Mrs Peploe sums up an account of it all thus, ' At every meal there were arguments on every subject. It was great fun listening.' Then the Russian Ballet came to Paris. Bakst used all the modern painting ideas for his *décor* and Diaghileff was to find his highest expectations amply exceeded. ' No wonder,' said J. D., ' that S. J. thought the nights at the ballet were among the greatest of his life. They were the greatest nights in anyone's life. Schéhérazade, Petroushka, Sacre du Printemps, Nijinsky, Karsavina and Fokine.' There were also the Cirque Medrano and a host of other excitements.

From 1910 and on into the early months of 1914 the Peploes spent most of their time more or less in France. With Paris as headquarters they made excursions to various places—Brittany, Royan, where the elder of their two sons was born, Cassis and other places on the Mediterranean coast. All during this happy phase, industry and enthusiasm

were maintained at a high level. S. J. was always aware of
the fact that he had a job of work to do and the days were
planned accordingly.   And there is no doubt that he was
well aware of what was happening to pictorial art in France
and had been so since his student days in Paris.   In the
intervening years he had kept up a correspondence with
Fergusson who, in long letters, discussed the latest phase,
telling him of Picasso and Braque and of what had grown
out of the ' Les Fauves ' phase of Matisse, Derain and others.
Of course S. J. in Edinburgh was very much intrigued, but
according to Fergusson there was no language for it that
made sense in London or Edinburgh.   Expressions like the
' logic of line and colour ' meant something in Paris but not
at home.   J. D. is of the opinion that even today most painters
in Britain do not fully understand what happened in Paris
before 1914.   Peploe certainly did and he knew it at first
hand.   Just as Wyndham Lewis was the first artist in England
who understood what the cubists and abstractionists generally
were trying to do, so do I think that Peploe was among the
first in Britain to make use of the ' researches ' of the post-
impressionist and the ' wild men ' who followed in their wake.

When he had returned to Paris with Margaret, his wife,
he found J. D. settled in the movement. He was taken by
him to see Picasso and together they attended the Salon
d'Automne dinner where they met Bourdelle, Friesz, Pascin
and others, and they sent pictures to the Salon d'Automne
exhibition.   It was under the various influences of this Paris
period that Peploe changed from ' blacks and greys ' to
colour and began to investigate the new ideas on design.
J. D. rejoiced in his company, for it was so much more
enchanting to be seeing things together instead of writing
about them.   But in the end Peploe elected to make his
permanent home in Scotland.

When Peploe returned to Edinburgh with the idea of a
great one-man show of his new work he found that he was
evidently very much in advance of public opinion.   McOmish

Dott, in whom sincere friendship fought a losing battle with the equally sincere convictions of the art dealer, simply could not face the prospect of being associated in any way with the new, raucous, exuberant kind of painting. For some time he had been gravely concerned over Peploe's 'changes' and was convinced that the influence of the Paris School was bound to be destructive. Indeed he had felt it his duty to write Mrs Peploe, imploring her not to shirk her responsibility. Her husband was a great artist, one of the few, and life and art in Paris were full of menace. She must see to it that he continued to paint the type of picture which his growing public could understand and would buy. Indeed, if Sam would just paint the flowers and 'things' which everybody loved to possess Aitken Dott's would buy them all and so on. Of course it was foolish counsel, even if kindly intended, for the young wife then as always would never dream of trying to exercise any direct influence on what or how her husband should paint.

Nevertheless the matter of an appreciative public, willing to demonstrate appreciation in the only effective way, was one of considerable importance. The one-man show was held in Shandwick Place. It created some stir, but the general view was that Peploe had run off the rails and that it was better to wait until he had run on again. Some stigmatised the new phase as sheer perversity. However, there were a few staunch supporters—notably John Ressich, the Glasgow business man, who was also a very able journalist, and in due time, not too long delayed, it was recognised that something new and worth while had happened to Scottish Art.

While the 1910 Post-impressionist Exhibition was not the first occasion whereby the English public could become aware of the great figures in French painting—the International Society had brought some over before then—it was important in creating a new conception of the function and purpose of pictorial art. It is true that the conception is not universally

59

accepted ; but in Scotland, at any rate, the work of the three Scottish colourists, led by Peploe, did much to help the interested public to understand that a painting is something more than a piece of interior decoration to be hung over the mantelpiece or sideboard. Moreover, when the writings of Roger Fry and Clive Bell began to drift North the interested could find the local illustrations for the ' new aesthetic ' in the new Scottish outlook.

From 1910 to 1914 should therefore be marked as the period when Peploe really discovered the line of approach to the problems of painting which he felt were worth solving. That does not mean to say that he settled down in a narrow groove in investigation or became insensitive to fresh experience. Trial and error alternated with periods of complete confidence and eminently satisfactory results. He would exploit the almost purely decorative quality of colour, and then become aware that his intellect was taking too strong a hold and that he might perhaps be restraining too much the urge to express himself emotionally. It is not easy to express the distinction clearly without reference to the actual paintings,. but if one compares the passage in Charles Marriott's *Modern Movements in Painting* with one's knowledge of Peploe's work as a whole the opinion may gain substance. Marriott is thinking of Fergusson and Peploe when he writes :

These painters are associated particularly with the *Fauve* or *Fauvist* movement. . . . They are before everything designers in paint in all three dimensions ; and they have adopted a style of boldly simplified and rhythmical drawing, bright colour pattern, and obvious and well organised brushwork which gives to their works a singularly robust appearance. Their designs are emphatic and closely articulated ; without any padding, and there is no hesitation in using a dark line instead of elaborate light and shade to relieve the forms. . . . It recalls the effects of stained glass.

Now that was written in 1926, but is applicable only to one phase of Peploe's work—a phase which is overshadowed by his more characteristic and less decorative work. Oddly

BOATS AT ROYAN   Oil 10½ × 14 in.

enough it appears to be the phase most remembered in the south.

When the 1914 War broke out Peploe immediately volunteered, but was found to be medically unfit for service. This depressed him considerably, for apart from the assault on his *amour-propre*, bearing in mind the soldierly dignity of his appearance, the discovery that he was physically below normal gave rise to a degree of anxiety. Added to that was the fact that the outbreak of war practically put an end to the sale of pictures. There was nothing for it, however, but to continue to paint and hope for the best. Reid at this time, and in the face of a completely unknown future, made the generous offer of a guaranteed annual income. And Peploe, while deeply appreciative and conscious of his responsibilities, preferred to retain a position of independence. It is certain that he was moved to this decision because of the fear that if he were under any obligation it would interfere with the freedom of action so essential to an artist.

The depression which had enveloped the business of art dealing did not last long. Reid held a Peploe exhibition in Glasgow in November 1915, and from then on sales were regular. Duncan Macdonald had moved to Edinburgh at the outbreak of war and in 1916 joined the Aitken Dott firm. He immediately became a Peploe enthusiast, and there are many today, including the writer, who rejoice that his enthusiasm was infectious. It was generally a case of turn about between Reid's and Aitken Dott in holding one-man shows of Peploe's paintings, and Macdonald took them farther afield to Dundee and Aberdeen. Later the custom of grouping him with Cadell and Hunter was developed.

The first post-war London show at the Leicester Gallery was in January 1923. There was no preface to the catalogue, only short biographical notes, and the exhibition was composed of thirty Cadells, twenty-nine Peploes and nineteen Hunters. The second Leicester Gallery show was two years later in January 1925, with the addition of J. D. Fergusson.

This time there were twelve Cadells, ten each by Peploe and Hunter and eight by J. D. who added three pieces of sculpture. Oliver Brown of the Leicester Gallery remembers that Sickert, whose etchings and engravings were being hung in another room, after viewing the Scots artists' paintings, volunteered to write a preface to the catalogue. It is thought that one reason for Sickert's gesture was in order that he might score off Roger Fry. In any case he made a fine salute to all four. This is what he wrote about Peploe :

Mr Peploe has carried a certain kind of delicious skill to a pitch of virtuosity that might have led to mere repetition, and his present orientation has certainly been a kind of rebirth. He has transferred his unit of attention from attenuated and exquisite graduations of tone to no less skilfully related colour. And by relating all his lines with frankness to the 180 degrees of two right angles, he is able to capture and digest a wider field of vision than before. And time, as the poet sings, is an important element in the gathering of roses. His *volte-face* has been an intellectual progress. And it is probably for this reason that, obviously beautiful as was Mr Peploe's earlier quality, his present one will establish itself as the more beautiful of the two.

Mr Brown recollects Hunter from his many visits, and that Cadell was very lively company, but he does not remember seeing anything of Peploe.

The two group exhibitions in Paris, one in 1924 at the Galeries Barbazanges and the other in 1931 at the Galeries Georges Petit, have been noted elsewhere. At the latter Telfer Bear and R. O. Dunlop were included. It was in a sense a gala performance, opened by Lord Tyrell, the British Ambassador to France, and the Prime Minister, Mr Ramsay MacDonald, wrote a foreword to the catalogue. Peploe had the unique honour of having a second painting—a Cassis landscape—purchased by the French Government.

Between the two Paris exhibitions in 1928 he had a show in the Kraushaar Galleries in New York. The thirty-two works which were shown were chiefly Iona seascapes, still-life and flowers, with one Cassis landscape. They represented him in his most personal style, and although the tangible results were not great he was on the whole well received. Moreover, he appears to have been in excellent spirits, if one may judge from the biographical notes he supplied for the catalogue. To his horror they appeared as written. Six years later the present writer was commissioned by the *Artist* to produce an article on Peploe for the ' Artists of Note ' series, and the only assistance he obtained from the ' victim ' was a blessing in the shape of ' Good Luck ! ' The memory of the Kraushaar foreword was evidently too much. Here it is :

Born Edinburgh, 1871, son of a banker, educated there, Edinburgh Collegiate School and University. Thought in turns of being a soldier, minister, indigo planter, lawyer, farmer and other pursuits, but preferred doing nothing as long as possible ; the ideal life is the lounger.

At the age of twenty (though not really tired of doing nothing) reading Carlyle and Ruskin was ' awakened ' to Art (a nice easy life, out-of-doors life). Got enthusiastic and worked hard ; went to Paris—Julien's under Bouguereau (damned old fool), then afterwards in Life School in Edinburgh. Took studio in Edinburgh, produced some masterpieces and a lot of failures. Continued like this till 1910 when married ; had to work hard. Family appeared—had to work harder still. At that time Paris (1911), a very lively time. Came home again, more family appeared—had to work really hard. This has gone on till present time.

There is no end to Art.

He took little or no part in either the initiation or the promotion of any of the exhibitions of his work. He left all propaganda and sales to his dealers, in whom he had complete faith. The business procedure was, to say the least of it, unusual, but it seldom varied. Whenever a sufficient number of paintings were completed, Peploe would arrange them round the wall of his studio. Reid, Macdonald or George Proudfoot, sometimes together or individually, would call, select the canvases they wished to buy, assemble them in a bunch and then depart. The following day a cheque for the total would be dispatched, Peploe would indicate approval and that was that. When I joined the Reid firm (now Reid & Lefevre) I inherited this method of acquiring Peploes, but the slump of 1929 coincided with my venture into the world of art, and it was not difficult to know the state of the picture market. It had practically ceased to exist. However, the Reid firm continued alone as buyers, and in due course I collected the studio key, Peploe took his walk, and I enjoyed the privilege of exercising my judgment in the time-honoured fashion. I also got to know the man. He must have had some doubts regarding this new-comer, but with his delightful whimsical smile he made one feel confident enough to express preferences and to give reasons for them. I think it was because I had included in my selection a glowing green landscape of New Abbey which had not previously found favour and which had moved me to expand on Constable—fresh from a concentrated study—that S. J. led me on until I was out of my depth. Be that as it may, in our all too infrequent meetings, it was easy to talk together without reservation. This is not common in art circles where every attempt to find virtue in men or their works seems always to be qualified by a ' but.'

Peploe resisted as much as he could all invitations to belong to any society or group. It was inevitable that the leading members of the Royal Scottish Academy should take due cognisance of the growing reputation of their contemporary. The older academicians were strongly in favour of his election. Sir James Guthrie, the President, James Paterson, the Secretary, and Charles Mackie gave a lead in requesting him to give serious consideration to the matter. He was, however, loath to assume responsibilities which might encroach on his freedom and he hated the thought of being involved in committee meetings, debates on policy or in attending functions. His attitude is, I think, beautifully

Plate V

TREES, ANTIBES   Oil 25 × 30 in.

Plate VI

ROSES AND FRUIT   Oil 22 × 20 in.

expressed in a letter he wrote in March 1918. It is addressed to another artist, Robert Rose :

I confess that at first the thing was to me rather a terrible shock : a setting-out, as it were, on a dangerous and difficult adventure, the end of which seemed hidden and quite impossible of realization.

I am by nature timid and fearful, lacking courage always seeing ahead the ruts and boulders on the path of action—I *nearly* gave in. I *almost* gave it up.

Then there dawned light, faint at first, but growing stronger, the light of conviction. It was to be for my good—I mean, really and truly for my good, my mental and spiritual good. It had to be.

By means of it I would become larger and more human. It seemed to offer at the moment just what I wanted. It was like a marriage. I felt the same before, I remember, on the eve of my marriage. ' I am going to give up my freedom, I am going to make chains to bind me.' Fear . . .

I know now that if there are chains of bondage there are also chains of love.

Real freedom *is* being bound. Giving up oneself to a purpose, an idea, something greater than self. The other freedom only ends in self-destruction.

To the mystics, freedom was obedience, fasting and prayer. By means of these to know God. Perfection. They are right.

It may seem funny to write like this because one has become an associate of the R.S.A., but that is how I see it.

Already I know it has done me good, it has linked me to others, it has vitalized me. Now I can go on.

O ! I envy you. The country just now, the warm sun, the spring flowers. You are fortunate.

Absorb it all, dear Rose. Just drink it in. It is life.

—Adieu, S. J. Peploe.

From the foregoing it is clear that the recipient was a man who enjoyed the full confidence of the writer. Robert Traill Rose was a Scottish artist (born in Newcastle), greatly esteemed by his contemporaries in literary and artistic Edinburgh. His work was largely in the field of book illustration, but his critical comments and kindliness endeared him to a large circle. Bunty Cadell was best man at his wedding, with S. J. supporting them both. The bonds of friendship between Rose and his friends grew closer as deafness and blindness began to shut him off from the normal channels of communication. Sustained by a devoted wife, he bore the double affliction with great fortitude. He died in 1942. It was Rose who put on record : ' These evenings with the Peploes ! like jewels in the dim past.'

In 1927 Peploe was elected to full membership of the Academy. Cadell did his utmost to persuade him to become a founder member of the Society of Eight but without success. Eventually he accepted honorary membership and sent occasionally to the annual exhibitions.

The Peploe and Cadell friendship was a rare thing. In appearance, manner and talk they were poles apart, but in their love of colour, sunshine and freedom of action they were on common ground. It was Cadell who, in 1920, persuaded Peploe to visit Iona where he seemed to find exactly what he had been looking for in the way of fresh adventure. For the next ten years Peploe devoted himself to capturing the island and the surrounding sea in all the various moods conditioned by weather changes. The technique he employed and the manner in which he continued the McTaggart tradition, have been brilliantly analysed by Stanley Cursiter. It is therefore enough to say here that in Iona Peploe enjoyed himself to the full, finding a great satisfaction in the gifts provided by nature and in creating pictures which won for him the enthusiastic appreciation of a growing public. Cadell was, as always, the witty delightful companion with his mimicry, light versifying and fund of merry anecdotes. His gay, generous and happy nature provided just the kind of atmosphere Peploe needed, and the family shared to the full all the joys of those great days in Iona. Back in Edinburgh, Cadell's studio was about the only one S. J. ever visited. They often criticised each other's work, suggesting an improvement here and there, counselling eliminations of some passage or advising a fresh attempt.

It was never easy to extract from him an observation on any artist's work, particularly if it did not appeal to him. Mrs Peploe recalls a visit which they paid together to a well-known contemporary's studio. After tea the host produced, one after another, examples of his work, obviously expecting some kind of comment. S. J., growing more uncomfortable as the demonstration continued, remained completely silent until the awkwardness of the situation became too much for his wife and they beat a hasty retreat.

He knew of and encouraged my enthusiasm for Hunter's work, for which he himself had a high regard. I remember a long and very pleasant afternoon in February 1932 when he came over to Glasgow to see Hunter's memorial exhibition and subjected almost every picture to a careful scrutiny. His remarks were illuminating and his analysis charged with understanding and sympathy. It was then, pointing to a painting of a houseboat on Loch Lomond, that he said, ' That is Hunter at his best and it is as fine as any Matisse.' Apart from the value of his opinion the fact that he expressed himself at all is important. Ion Harrison has noted elsewhere that Peploe's reluctance to comment on the work of a contemporary was related to the theory that no practising artist can possibly hold an unbiased opinion. The bias in another direction is obvious in his own work.

When he was persuaded in 1933 to give some of his time to teaching in the Edinburgh College of Art the surprise at the news was more than balanced by the conviction that his influence would be of the utmost service to the rising generation. It is clear now that this sense of duty and his loyalty to the idea that Scotland could and should make advances in art endeavour were strained beyond his physical resources and peace of mind. While he applied himself faithfully to the task he had undertaken he was not happy. Indeed, the effort to adapt himself to the requirements of class teaching assumed the character of an ordeal and he began to feel that he was temperamentally unsuited and altogether ineffective.

In this he was wrong, because his presence and the high regard and respect in which he was held by the student body, gave to the slightest of his comments or criticisms an authority which was in every way outstanding. Perhaps there came into his mind the pronouncement of Whistler : ' I don't teach art, with that I cannot interfere ; but I teach the scientific application of paint and brushes,' and Peploe might have felt that the teacher himself has to be trained to teach. The value of his short period of teaching lay in the example of his own career and some of his students would certainly be brought to realise that an artist sees through the progressive practice of his art and that perception is related to personality rather than to hard and accurate fidelity to a selected theme. And it is equally certain he left the impression that there is no easy road to perfection.

Many of his completed canvases have what appears to be tentative essays or abandoned efforts on the reverse side. This practice was not peculiar to Peploe, but very few artists have left so much clear evidence of self-criticism. We have already noted that unlike Hunter, and to some extent Cadell, he regarded his intellect as of greater value than his inspiration. He was often harassed with doubts and was always extremely modest about himself and his work. Although it pleased and surprised him to find people liked him, neither himself nor his paintings were permitted as a topic of conversation in his presence.

Peploe's approach to life was detached but not contemptuous. He hated violence of thought, speech or action. He treated his mind as a divine thing, refusing to permit it to be controlled by any sect, school or regulation. Considerate and courteous as he was, uncharitable gossip, pretension or humbug drove him into silence. This sometimes made him unpopular with some of his fellow-artists who looked upon his aloofness as an assumption of superiority, but when the privilege of his friendship was won his innate modesty and quiet dignity were recognised as chief among his

Plate I

HEAD OF A BOY   Oil 22 × 20 in.

Plate 2

MELON, GRAPES AND APPLES   Oil 16 × 20 in.

Plate 3

LOAF AND JUG   Oil 20 × 16 in.

Plate 4

ROSES IN CHINA VASE   Oil 20 × 16 in.

Plate 5

THE PINE TREES   Oil 16 × 13 in.

Plate 6

TULIPS   Oil 24 × 20 in.

Plate 7

STREET IN CASSIS   Oil 12½ × 16 in.

Plate 8

STREET SCENE, FRANCE

Oil $13\frac{1}{2} \times 10\frac{1}{2}$ in.

charming qualities. He had no eccentricities and never manifested anything in the nature of bohemian peculiarities. In his home, which he loved, he could relax in an atmosphere of comfort and perfect understanding. S. J. shared his mind, his work and his happiness with his wife and two sons. When he did surrender to an invitation to lunch or dinner or had spent an evening in Bunty Cadell's studio, he would store up the incidents and features of the occasion, minor and major, and retail them with good-humoured jest when he returned home.

His tall, lean upright figure gave him a commanding appearance, quite unlike the general conception of what an artist should look like. He did not affect anything out of the ordinary in his clothes, but he was meticulous in the matter of cut and style and his tailor had to produce the perfect garment even if it remained unworn for quite a time. Interest in dress was not absorbing. Rather was it a further indication that he abhorred anything slip-shod in the making, and he had a masculine affection for old and trusty garments. These he wore with such distinction that an observer in Iona was heard to say, ' Mr Peploe looks well-dressed in his old clothes—even when they are splashed with paint.'

The closing years of his life were marred with illness. He tried to keep on working in spite of an overpowering lassitude and continued to be represented in the R.S.A. and the Glasgow Institute. Reid & Lefevre held an exhibition in March 1934, his last London show. After his death in October 1935, memorial exhibitions were held in Edinburgh and Glasgow. Sir James Caw wrote a foreword to one catalogue and E. A. Taylor to the other. Both of these were fitting tributes to Peploe as man and artist. Press and public alike confirmed his right to the high place he had won for himself in his lifetime in the history of Scottish Art.

It is true that the full meed of his success was not vouchsafed to him when he could have enjoyed it, but such appears to be the common lot of men who merit the title great.   Peploe now belongs to the ages and to those who prefer to await the *cachet* conferred by death, but there were some who esteemed his worth when he was alive.   And they too have their reward in the satisfying evidence of a man revered by his succeeding generation and of an artist whose name and work have become part of our national heritage.

F. C. B. Cadell
1883–1937

F. C. B. Cadell

F. C. B. Cadell

1883–1937

FRANCIS CAMPBELL BOILEAU CADELL was born in Edinburgh on the 12th April 1883. He was the eldest son of Dr Francis Cadell and his wife, Mary Hamilton Boileau. The Cadells are an old Edinburgh family with a Lothian background, and mostly associated in the past with the Army, civil service or law. There does not appear to have been any forbear for whom an artistic inheritance may be claimed. Dr Cadell was a graduate of Edinburgh University and practised medicine in the capital for many years. He died in 1909.

Through his father's side of the family Cadell had links with the west. Lady George Campbell of Strachur was a cousin, and in another Campbell link he was distantly related to the Duke of Argyll. The late Principal Storey of Glasgow University was also a relative and, through the distaff side, the family of Principal Lindsay of the Free Church College has a distant link with the Cadells. That line would therefore lead us to the Master of Balliol. The genealogical tree has many roots and branches, but beyond stating the obvious that Cadell's mother was of French extraction—her family originally came from Nîmes—we shall leave further details to a fuller biography.

Dr Cadell had one other son, Colonel A. P. H. Cadell who served in the Indian Army, and a daughter, the well-known stage and film actress, Miss Jean Cadell. The mention of Jean Cadell's name brings to mind the Glasgow Repertory Theatre movement, where she counted among her associates several young players who, like herself, have achieved fame and distinction in their profession.

73

F. C. B. was educated at Edinburgh Academy, but there is no record of any special scholastic attainment. There is a family legend that Cadell began to draw when he was two years old. He used his left hand, and nothing was done to persuade him to adopt the supposedly orthodox practice of drawing with his right. It is perhaps more correct to say that one oblique attempt was made and dealt with, in accordance with the story Cadell was fond of telling when anyone remarked on his unusual methods. When a student in the Royal Scottish Academy life school the President stood watching Cadell for a little and then said, ' Young man, you will never become an artist if you paint with your left hand. No artist ever became great who did so.' Cadell straightened up and replied, ' Sir, and did not the great Michelangelo paint with his left hand ? ' The President gave a grunt, turned on his heel and walked off. When the inevitable question was asked, ' And did Michelangelo paint with his left hand ? ' Cadell would reply with a twinkle, ' I haven't the slightest idea ; but neither had the President.'

It is clear that he had a peculiar talent which was recognised and encouraged. He did not have to resist parental obstruction, and some credit for this must be given to Arthur Melville, a leading member of the group of artists who created ' The Glasgow School ' when Cadell was learning how to walk and talk. Melville, who was an intimate friend of the family (Cadell's younger brother is his godson), saw some of the child's drawings, and observed that the young artist appeared to know instinctively what most people had to go to Art School to learn. The drawings still survive and were exhibited in a retrospective exhibition in April 1942.

It is interesting to record that Arthur Melville exercised considerable influence on the career of another notable Scottish colourist, J. D. Fergusson. In his book, *Modern Scottish Painting*, J. D. writes : ' He [Melville] was my first influence. Although I never met him or even saw him, his painting gave me my first start : his work opened up to me the way of free painting—not merely freedom in the use of paint but freedom in outlook.'

It has to be noted that Cadell's father was not indifferent to art. Indeed, he was a man of taste with a flair for recognising worth-while endeavour. Melville was bold enough to advise Dr Cadell not to submit his son to art teaching as ordinarily understood, but to send him to Paris when he was about fifteen. This counsel was accepted in part and Cadell eventually worked in various Paris studios, including Julien's, from 1899 to 1903. It has to be added that his mother sacrificed everything to ensure that her son received the best available instruction. She lived in Paris with F. C. B. and his sister Jean for three years. She also spent some time with them in Munich, where she died in 1907.

The earlier pictures, following a wide range of interesting efforts in his boyhood, were painted under a strong impressionist influence. There was nothing revolutionary in his pictorial outlook, and he had the distinction of ' a picture in the Salon ' when he was sixteen. Although he came into contact with the vital Post-impressionist surge in French painting at an age which is supposed to be peculiarly sensitive, Cadell was less permanently influenced than were Peploe and Hunter. He always retained a much wider range of interest in what he considered paintable material. Certainly he had his preferences, but any subject was grist to his mill.

Cadell eventually returned to Edinburgh in 1909, and from then onwards he made his home in Scotland. He paid occasional visits to France and spent one memorable period in Venice. This Venice visit of some months' duration was made possible through the generosity of Sir Patrick Ford, a life-long friend.

Later, some of his reactions to Army life and personnel are wittily recorded in a volume published by Grant Richards, *Jack and Tommy*. Of the numerous original sketches, sixteen are in the Harrison Collection. When these topical comments are related to his more serious work two conclusions are warranted. Cadell from his early youth must have had a quick eye and a nimble wit, qualities which were made manifest in his conversation as well as in his finest paintings. His self-assurance and complete independence sometimes led the casual observer to look upon his eccentricities as sheer vanity if not selfishness. As a matter of fact he loved good company, clean and rich living, if and when available, and he chose to make his contribution in a manner which was original, surprising and effective. In dress, speech, company, work and play he was never dull. It was impossible not to laugh with him. His gaiety was infectious, and to be in his company was an excellent antidote to despondency.

His friends called him 'Bunty,' and he was known and spoken of as Bunty Cadell in a large circle of acquaintances who found delight in his paintings or in his adventures and witticisms. In Scotland 'Bunty' is much more than a nickname. It is a term of endearment, and the bearer of it is always assured that his qualities are more than sufficient to obliterate his failings. It is often said of an artist that he refuses to be bound by regulations and rules, and, when it is said, one is thinking of his work rather than of his conduct or of his attitude to life. With Cadell the application becomes general. In work, in play, in speech or letter-writing, in small or large gatherings he was himself. He never 'put on an act.' If he appeared to do so the observer would eventually reach the conclusion, 'This is a bit of Bunty that I never knew before.'

When war was declared in 1914 Cadell volunteered immediately. To his surprise and dismay he was turned down because of 'smoker's heart.' He stopped smoking—no mean feat, for a pipe was seldom out of his mouth—and worked on a farm in Galloway until he was fit to pass the doctor. A commission had no attraction for him, and it was only under pressure from his C.O. that he latterly became an officer in the Argyll and Sutherland Highlanders.

When he joined up and was posted to the Royal Scots he

Plate I

THE WHITE ROOM   Oil 25 × 30 in.

abhorred his readymade tommy's uniform and had a well-cut
replica made of really good material by his expensive Edinburgh tailor. On occasion he would parade in this, out of
barracks, but when his own sergeant saluted him he narrowly
escaped a court-martial. He withstood all the rigours and
discomforts of warfare on the Somme and elsewhere, was
twice wounded, and throughout the whole period of service
adapted himself cheerfully to every circumstance.

When the days of uniform had passed he very quickly
returned to his dashing style of dress. On his first day of
' civvies ' he was walking along Princes Street when he heard
a small boy remark, ' My ! it's a peety some things is
demobilised.' Cadell's best stories and quips were generally
against himself. He decorated his person and his surroundings according to his fancy with deliberation and disregard
for criticism. But he was never deaf to the comments aroused
by such behaviour. Indeed he enjoyed hearing them. In
Iona, where he spent so many happy and productive summers,
the residents would whisper as Cadell approached in all his
tartan finery, kilt and silk shirt, ' Here's Himself.' He knew
it. His boisterous, aggressive good nature and his gaiety were
just his way of saying, ' Oh, what a beautiful morning,
everything's going my way.'

And if, sometimes, things did not go his way, he accepted
adversity as the necessary shade, essential to give quality to
the light. It is because Cadell's paintings reveal the man in
the artist—and this can be more truly said of him than of
Peploe or Hunter—that the nature of his light-heartedness
and humour is so well worth recording and indeed empha-
sising. His wit was of the Rabelaisian order, sometimes
macabre, but never distasteful. It was never ponderous. It
came in a flash. Many of his *bons mots* have become conversa-
tional currency ; indeed some have found it convenient to
forget that Cadell first coined them. Soon after he went to
study in Paris the President of France, Félix Faure, died
suddenly. There was a discussion between Cadell and a

friend as to whether they would go to a private view of paintings or to the lying-in-state of Félix Faure. 'Let's make it the lying-in-state,' said Cadell. 'The pictures will keep, but the President won't.'

The great influx of visitors to Iona in the summer frequently puts an excessive strain on the island's water supply. A visitor had been lamenting to Cadell that he had been on the island for a fortnight and had been unable to get a bath. He was met with the retort, 'Didn't you know? In Iona you either stink or swim!'

Of course Cadell did not have exclusive rights to Iona as a painting ground. Indeed he introduced many of his contemporaries—notably Peploe—to the loveliness of the island and the inexhaustibility of its supply of motifs. It is a painter's paradise, and those with a more academic outlook found their own satisfaction in attempting to transfer its beauty on to canvas. But Cadell was by common consent acknowledged as the chief representative of the fraternity of artists. His independence and irrepressibility were occasionally sources of exasperation. Returning one day from a spell of painting in one of the bays, Cadell passed an artist who was engaged in painting the Cathedral, apparently stone by stone, and with meticulous care—spending weeks in the process. He remarked to Cadell, 'Surely you haven't finished your picture already!' 'Certainly,' was the reply. 'It took me a couple of hours, and I've sold it too — for a hundred guineas.' 'You're cheating the public,' remonstrated the other, 'a picture painted in two hours isn't worth tenpence!' Cadell has done a delightful caricature of this particular Iona companion, with the caption, 'X putting the finishing touches to a water-colour started in 1900.'

Sir James Barrie's play *The Boy David* had its première in Edinburgh in 1936. Cadell's sister Jean was playing in it and Bunty attended with his friend, Sir Patrick Ford. In one scene, before the fight between David and Goliath, an army of brawny Philistines, stripped to the waist, appeared

on the stage.   Sir Patrick whispered to his companion,
' What's the big idea—this half-naked army ? '   Cadell
retorted in a flash, ' Wheesht ! they've put their shirts on
David.'

Cadell never married, but he was never indifferent to
feminine charm and loveliness.   And he was devoted to
children.   They loved him and they also respected him.   He
was a great playmate, but with the subtle sense peculiar to
children they apprehended the ' great ' as something just
above an ordinary level.   This is perhaps reflected in another
Iona incident.   Cadell was there in the off-season when the
population was scanty.   Two children, playing near their
mother in a quiet deserted bay, saw a figure approaching in
the distance.   One remarked to the other, ' There's a man
coming.'   ' That's not a man,' was the retort, ' that's
Mr Cadell ! '   His nephew, John Percival Clark (better
known now as John Cadell since he adopted his mother's
maiden name when he decided to continue in the family
stage tradition), had a special admiration for his uncle.   He
found the utmost delight in the stories which were invented
for his special benefit.   Uncle ' Bunty's ' narratives of the
famous Mrs Scroggan with the tartan face—the lady who
always wore an alarm clock on her chest and had such
amazing adventures are for ever remembered.

How exciting things were sure to be if one were taken on
an expedition along Princes Street, ending up in a tea-
room with the certainty of an original and fantastic dialogue
with the waitress.   The pretence that there was no money
and the vision of a night in gaol ! Nothing terrifying about
it all—the condemned cell even, if Uncle Bunty was there,
would be an attractive place to continue the make-believe.
Cadell could extract the last ounce of value from ' once upon
a time.'

He could also create the situation capable of acquiring
a fairy-tale flavour.   When Lord Tweedsmuir, then John
Buchan, was High Commissioner at the Church of Scotland

Assembly, Cadell was invited to the reception. Mrs Buchan who was seated on the throne picked Cadell out from the crowd and suggested to her husband that he should insist that Cadell should occupy the adjoining throne. In the course of conversation Mrs Buchan said that she was dying for a cigarette, but that she supposed she daren't. Cadell said, ' Madam, for the time being you are a queen and you can do anything.' He produced his case and offered her a cigarette. When she had lit up she said to Cadell, ' But you are not smoking.' He observed that he didn't smoke cigarettes but a pipe, and that it would hardly do to smoke a pipe. Mrs Buchan immediately said, ' For the time being I am the queen, and I order you to smoke your pipe.' This explains the extraordinary incident of Cadell sitting in the Throne Room of Holyrood Palace smoking a pipe. He said afterwards that he felt like Old King Cole.

The fund of Cadell anecdotes and witticisms is almost inexhaustible. A selection is quoted because in some measure they reflect the man. In this he stands out in clear contrast to Peploe and Hunter. It is not possible to talk of Bunty Cadell to anyone who knew him without being reminded of this or that occasion when he was the chief actor. Perhaps it is too easy, and not very convincing, to perceive in his outlook as an artist and in his approach to any fresh adventure in painting, the character of the individual as manifested in his attitude to life, men and affairs. At the same time it is difficult to separate his care-free way of living from the spontaneity of his best work.

In his letters one also finds evidence of a quick reaction to incident and circumstance. He was not a great corre-spondent, nor was he possessed of the contemplative mind, but it would be wrong to conclude that he was incapable of making a careful analysis of people, place, situation, book or current topic. It was simply that he placed a greater reliance on the spontaneous reaction, because it aroused more fun than did the careful patient study of the ordinary

RT BHAN, IONA   Oil 14½ × 17½ in.

Plate III

MRS ION R. HARRISON

Oil 30 × 25 in.

things in life. This explains in some measure the nature of his versatility. There was nothing of the bohemian in his make-up. Adventures had their fascination, but they must not be experienced at the expense of personal comfort or conducted at too great a distance from a hot bath and an aperitif.

He was an egoist, but an amiable egoist. When one got to know him, it became clear that his apparent self-idolatry was really self-sufficiency. Probably he paraphrased Coleridge to fit his own conceptions :

> O Lady, we receive but what we give
> And in our lives alone doth nature live.

Cadell painted a great number of pictures in Iona. He went there every summer for twenty years. In oils and water-colours, with brush and pencil, he produced landscapes, portraits, still life, interiors, caricatures and sketches of all kinds. Periods of idleness alternated with spells of furious energy, but he was never inaccessible and whatever and wherever the company he was the central figure.

Apart from one-man shows held in the premises of different dealers in Edinburgh and Glasgow, Cadell's work was to be seen with fair regularity at the Royal Scottish Academy exhibitions in the summer, and at the Fine Art Institute in Glasgow in the autumn. He took an active part in the activities of the Society of Eight, and was one of its founder members. This Society of Eight was created in 1912 by the following : P. W. Adam, David Alison, F. C. B. Cadell, James Cadenhead, John Lavery, Harrington Mann, James Paterson and A. G. Sinclair. Harrington Mann resigned a few years later and was succeeded by W. Y. Macgregor. It will be noted that most of them had received or were to receive academic honours, and that Lavery is unique in being the only member of the English Royal Academy. Later on S. J. Peploe, John Duncan, H. J. Lintott, W. G. Gillies and Arch. McGlashan were elected to fill vacancies which occurred during Cadell's life-time.

Cadell appears to have been more interested in the Society of Eight and its exhibitions than in any other art institution. He often claimed that the ' average ' was at a much higher level than could be seen elsewhere. Whether it was that he felt a sense of personal responsibility in the company of kindred minds or conceived it his duty to act as honorary publicist is not easy to determine. At the annual exhibition of the Society each member, and an occasional guest, had a space for as many as twenty works allotted to him. It is certain that Cadell took pains to ensure that he would be represented by his best work. He was much more indifferent or casual on other occasions. Probably he was fully aware of the distinction to be made between the selected exhibition of paintings with certain recognised standards and the larger fashionable affairs where the standards were unrecognisable, or at least impossible to define. Although sales were always matters of importance to him, with the Society of Eight he concentrated on having a selection of some works which had passed into private collections and which he thought important examples.

In matters of business Cadell was anything but sound. Sometimes he would price his paintings with a complete disregard of market values or of the chances of any dealer finding a customer. The dealer was instructed that canvases or water-colours which he thought represented him at the top of his form must not be sold below a fixed sum. When the work was returned to the studio it was more than likely that a purchaser would soon be found by Cadell himself, but at half the original ' fixed ' price. Unlike Peploe and Hunter, Cadell did not leave the sale of pictures entirely to the art dealers, and although the latter were sometimes exasperated to the point of non-co-operation there was never any ill-will. To criticise his irresponsibility was easy ; to quarrel with him was impossible.

If art criticism as a profession had made any appeal to him, it is more than probable that Cadell would have made his mark. At times he could be scathing, but he was also generous in appreciation. And his inherent courtesy could always bridge the awkward silences when diametrically opposed views were in conflict. His general attitude to painting and art institutions is revealed in some passages from his correspondence with Ion Harrison. These excerpts are taken at random from some letters written at infrequent intervals between the years 1929 and 1936.

I've finished ' Whistler' and enjoyed it very much. He was a marvellous painter, the most exquisite of the ' moderns ' and he had what some great painters have, a certain ' amateurishness ' which I rather like and felt always in Gainsborough. I can best describe what I mean in these words, ' A gentleman painting for his amusement.' (Of course it must be understood that the said ' gentleman ' is a genius as well !) This subject might be enlarged upon, for this quality or defect (whichever you like to call it in great painters) is exceedingly rare. Whistler certainly had it and so had Gainsborough. Raeburn on the other hand was a ' professional ' if ever there was one. I have never heard the subject discussed and I haven't the slightest idea if birth and early environment have anything to do with it. Probably not.

No. 6 Ainslie Place is the Edinburgh address which I associate most closely with Cadell. My first visit to him there was in November 1929 shortly after I had joined Reid & Lefevre (having succumbed to the invitation from A. J. McNeill Reid and Duncan Macdonald to abandon the smooth practice of medicine for the ups and downs of art dealing). The cleanest and tidiest studios I have ever seen were those of Cadell and J. D. Fergusson (in Paris). The former had his faithful man-servant Charles to look after him. J. D. did for himself. Come weal or woe, affluence or privation, Cadell refused to part with Charles, or it may have been the other way about. Certainly Charles (no-one ever seems to have known his other name) was the complete expert in domestic affairs. Moreover, he had opinions to offer on people and affairs in general and in art Cadell confessed quite seriously that Charles's views on pictures were infinitely more sound and reliable than those by ' critics ' who were supposed to know. In the postscript of a letter dated April 1932 is this :

I have not yet had Charles' opinion on *Genesis* [Epstein's large work] but I await it with interest. I think a wireless talk on the subject between Charles and Reid should be arranged by the B.B.C. [Reid was Harrison's chauffeur.]

The earliest in the package of letters which Ion Harrison has placed at my disposal is dated 1st December 1929 from Ainslie Place. Two extracts are of particular interest :

Some people *will buy* old pictures, but many unfortunately do not buy good ones or genuine examples. . . . The advantage in buying modern pictures is (1) that the buyer knows the work to be by the artist who paints it ; (2) buying comparatively low, with the sporting chance, combined with either knowledge or luck, that the pictures will go up, and (3) the advantage—and this to the painter—of encouraging contemporary art without which there would be no future ' old masters.' . . .

If your son ever has to ' raise the wind,' which I hope will not be the case, he will find your Peploe's most useful. A splendid investment. If I were a rich man I'd buy a lot of them even if I couldn't hang them all.

In March 1933 Cadell moved from Ainslie Place to 30 Regent Terrace. He writes from there :

At long last I write, having been frightfully busy getting into this very charming house—overlooking Holyrood and with a splendid and almost highland view of Arthur's Seat. A perfect prospect for a town house from which I'll get a good view of the doings of my friend Iain Colquhoun in May. [Sir Iain Colquhoun was Lord High Commissioner for that year's General Assembly of the Church of Scotland.] . . . I was so sorry not to be able to come through for the Hunter Show [a memorial exhibition : Hunter had died in 1931] but it was impossible. Reid & Lefevre are having a show of the

Plate IV

THE HARBOUR, CASSIS

Oil 18 × 15 in.

' Scottish Group ' in London. Macdonald is coming here today or tomorrow to choose pictures of mine for it. I always prefer this to choosing them myself as salesmen can sell so much better what they like themselves.

. . . Poor Hunter ! I suppose he will be well represented at the forthcoming London Show. I look forward to seeing your new ones. I always admired his work—more especially his still life and lighter quick sketches.

The marvellous outlook at Regent Terrace did not ensure a constant state of well-being :

Things are hellish, and if one fine day you see me sitting at Maule's corner with an upturned Lincoln Bennet don't be too surprised to drop a penny in it. Such is life ! Who wants a future one—what an inducement to Christianity—a man on a thing that sounds like a fog-horn is blowing ' Hark the Herald Angels ' outside the house as I write—Blast him !

In the early 1930s following the economic slump artists in Scotland, as elsewhere, were having a thin time. Cadell comments upon the changed days thus :

By the way do you remember my telling you about that picture Oldham wanted to buy ? Well, I have just sold it to Rochdale for £190. Good for Lancs !

Academies are constantly being criticised for their sins of omission and their tardiness in bestowing honours where honours are due. There are generally two sides to the question. In Edinburgh, and in London too, factors other than distinction in art are bound to operate. As in Clubs, so in Academies ; the powers that be are equally sensitive to irrelevancies in accepting or rejecting candidates. Belatedly, it is true, Cadell was elected an A.R.S.A. in 1931. He replies to Harrison's letter of congratulation :

Many thanks ! I do not ' care two hoots '—not one ! Lavery wrote to me asking me to convey his congratulations to the R.S.A. who had ' at last seen the light.' But to do the moribund body justice they are not altogether to blame ; for in a tantrum of temper I took my name off the waiting list just after the war, and it was only with great persuasion I was induced to put it on again a fortnight before the recent election, so that it is really a record of speed !

This matter of academic honours and awards is a vexed question, and it is as wrong as it is unfair to make generalisations from particular cases. The Royal Academy is criticised harshly in every fresh account of John Constable's life and career, but merit has never been the sole criterion in election to academic honour. How can it be? The most deserving either in academic or non-academic opinion may have given clear indications that the honour is not coveted. They may eventually be persuaded, as in Cadell's and other cases. The high quality of work may be lost sight of because of personal unpopularity or because adverse criticism of the institution concerned has been too forceful to live down. The unfortunate sequel is that academic honours in Art cannot be regarded as the essential mark of excellence. It has been noted that Cadell was elected A.R.S.A. in 1931. He was made an R.S.W. in 1935 and a full R.S.A. in 1936. He died in 1937. It may be said, therefore, that official recognition came to him late in life, but it is clear that it could have been otherwise had he so wished it.

Apart from actual honours, Cadell was always certain of representation in the annual exhibitions of the various art institutions. His first exhibited picture was a small water-colour which was accepted by the Paris Salon in 1899—when he was sixteen. It is now in the collection of Mrs Percival Clark (Jean Cadell). In 1902 he had two pictures—a portrait and a Paris landscape—in the Royal Scottish Academy. These were relegated to the ' condemned cell,' a small room generally reserved for the eccentrics or the beginners. Its equivalent in the Glasgow Institute was dubbed ' The Chamber of Horrors.' In the same year he exhibited in the Society of Scottish Artists, and thereafter exhibited in Edinburgh and Glasgow with great regularity. He also held one-man shows either at Aitken Dott or Doig

Wilson & Wheatly in Edinburgh or at Reid's in Glasgow. After Reid's had transferred their business to London, Cadell continued with Pearson & Westergaard who acted as his Glasgow agent.

The last three years of Cadell's life were far from comfortable. A series of accidents incapacitated him from time to time but failed to affect his lightness of heart. The first to be recorded is at the end of 1934 when he writes :

A fortnight ago I fell down the stairs of one of our infernal tramcars and landed on the tail of my spine on one of their metal-edged steps. Since when I have been unable to do anything but stand up. I have also developed deafness in my right ear—temporary I hope— though it may be the beginning of the end !

Later on he injured his ankle and then his knee—irritating incapacities which made it difficult either to get around or to concentrate on work. But in spite of the discomfort he managed to do both. Then he developed antrum trouble, which was generally supposed to be the sequel to a vicious attack by some hooligan outside his house in Regent Terrace. This led to a series of operations. After the first he went off by himself to the Highlands, feeling wretched. He sent a postcard of a beautiful spot near Morar to his sister, with these words, ' This lovely place has no more effect on me than Queen Street Station, Glasgow—so you know that I must really be resting.' The final illness appears to have been of a more deep-rooted character, requiring major surgical treatment which proved unavailing. He suffered a great deal of pain, but endeavoured to entertain his attendants and visitors with quip and jest until within a few hours of his death. It could truly be said of him that his courage never lost its occupation nor his face its smile.

The following letter appeared in *The Scotsman* two days later :

SIR,—By a singular and fitting coincidence Brahms's Pianoforte Concerto in D minor, said to have been inspired by the tragic illness and death of a great musician, was played here last night, but a few

hours after the death of one of Edinburgh's most distinguished men
—Mr F. C. B. Cadell.

To those who knew him and his work the first and second movements were poignant ; and the third, with its vigour, brilliance and
fun, brought him also to our saddened thoughts.—I am, etc.,

' MUSICIAN.'

Arthur Schnabel was the soloist. It is fitting, I think, to let
this anonymous letter represent the obituary notices which
are fleeting in their effect and try to find in his work the
memories which endure.

Apart from snippets of conversation and correspondence,
Cadell, as far as I have been able to discover, never indulged
much in theorising about art. He would discuss it freely,
and often subjected paintings, good, bad and indifferent, to
a searching analysis. But his general attitude was rather,
' Well, if that is how he sees it, why should I worry ? '

Constable once said he was anxious that the world should
look to painters for information on painting. Cadell had no
such anxiety, not because he suffered from any poverty of
language, but because he did not think it was the artist's
business. He read and listened to critics, but their utterances
were accepted rather as entertainment than as education.

Tomorrow night I go to a lecture by Roger Fry on Modern Art,
which should be quite interesting. 8.30 a fairly reasonable time.
Most evening entertainments in Scotland seem to be arranged for
people who indulge in ' High Tea.'

It is certain that in the society of artists Cadell would take a
prominent part in discussion on the purpose and function of
art, and in the aims and techniques of artists. He would
respect earnest differences of opinion. He had, for example,
a high regard for Peploe's intellect, but in the long run he
would certainly reach the opinion that great and mediocre
artists alike are capable of holding and of expressing the same
high ideals and the same sound judgments. Michelangelo
felt called upon to defend himself against the charge of
unsociability. ' There are many,' he once wrote, ' who

Plate V

INTERIOR, CROFT HOUSE

Oil 24 × 20 in.

maintain a thousand lies, and one is that eminent painters are strange, harsh and unbearable in their manners, although they are really human and humane.' Cadell would have been the last to claim eminence for himself. His first job, as an artist, was to be human and humane, not with calculation but simply because it was no part of his duty to change what the Almighty had ordered. He might have said with Michelangelo, ' Beauty was given at my birth to serve as my vocation's faithful exemplar,' and he carried his ideas of beauty into everything he touched. He decorated himself and his surroundings. In this he was unique.

I have in my time met a great number of artists. Most of them were physiologically and psychologically normal. Many of them seemed to abhor soap and water and elected to live in dirty and squalid surroundings—not because they had to, but because it did not occur to them that personal appearance or clean and tidy homes were of special importance. Hunter had to be provoked by the demands of a special occasion to pay any attention to his person or studio. Peploe's study was always clean and orderly but furnished only with the bare necessities. His wife saw to his comfort in a delightful home, and it would have embarrassed him beyond measure to wear anything out of the ordinary in clothes. Although not the complete sybarite, Cadell was certainly prone to luxurious living. We have seen that he enjoyed first-class quality in clothing, and wherever and whenever it was possible he made his surroundings conform to his idea of decoration. He liked people and places to be beautiful, and if they were not it was his vocation to make them so. To paint pictures was not enough. One had to express one's idea of decoration in everything. He made his studio a work of art. In a letter to Cadell, J. J. Cowan (one of his Edinburgh friends and patrons) writes :

John Duncan was with me at lunch yesterday and agreed with me that the open door between your studio and the approach thereto is one of the very best of your pictures.

When he rented a cottage in Iona, the first thing he did was to pack up the ' pictures ' on the wall and the odds and ends of ornaments. His sister once remonstrated with him, ' You shouldn't do this, you'll hurt Mrs X's feelings.' To which Bunty retorted, ' What about my feelings. I have to live here.'

It was in Iona that Cadell lived his fuller life as an artist. And it is to his work there that the Scottish colour-tradition label may be most fittingly applied. Perhaps some of his Iona paintings fall short of his initial conception in their rather slapdash handling. But it is in these that one sees a response to the essential qualities, a response which is powerful enough to push aside, as it were, the casual detached attitude discernible in some of his work where there is little more than clever, competent expression. He could be too light-hearted, and his daring did not always lead to a successful conclusion ; nevertheless his dynamic personality gave such variety to his pictorial language that his friends and patrons were always interested in the next thing he might be attempting. This is reflected in the number of collectors who kept adding to the Cadells in their possession. ' Something different from the last ' was irresistible. The late G. W. Service is an outstanding example. He was, by far, Cadell's greatest patron. Over a number of years he absorbed much of Cadell's output, and in his town house in Glasgow, and at his summer residence at Cove, paintings by Cadell were in every room.

This concentration on the art of one man may not commend itself to the average picture-lover blessed with the necessary means, but I can vouch for the fact that it was anything but a wearisome experience to inspect the Cadells in the Service collection. Moreover, the catalogues of the exhibition held in the National Gallery, Edinburgh, in 1942 will supply further evidence of collectors who were keen to possess more than one example. Ion Harrison has found that although each of the colourists Peploe, Cadell and

Hunter has his own individuality, when their works are hung together they present a unity which is eminently satisfying on the level of decoration without detracting from the particular values inherent in a work of art. We have noted that Cadell was the master of the agreeable art of swift response, but in his finest paintings we perceive seriousness of purpose strong enough to lift them to the realm of superb achievement.

Looking back at this distance one becomes aware of certain doubts. Some of us may have done an injustice to Cadell in minimising his special contribution. His vivid personality was apt to intrude itself between picture and spectator. It was too easy to believe that Bunty so enjoyed the art of living that he cared less for the job of picture making, that his work was incidental rather than compelling. Perhaps it was part of his fun to make us think so. Maybe his expression of delight when he saw again some of his earlier efforts also made one think that he had become less sure of his artistic integrity. On reflection and with an assurance which comes from recent surveys of his wide range of production, one is led to the conviction that Cadell is perhaps more truly Scottish than had hitherto been supposed. Although it has already been suggested that he was less permanently influenced by the revolutionary trends which operated at the beginning of the century it should not be forgotten that he was completely informed on all that was happening. As things are at present he may not be abreast of Peploe and Hunter in the rise towards a more universal appreciation as measured by market values, but in any account of Scottish painting these three artists will be inseparable.

Plate 1

THE PINK AZALEAS   Oil 24 × 18 in.

Plate 2

REFLECTIONS

Oil 25 × 30 in.

Plate 3

THE SACRISTY DOOR, IONA   Oil 30 × 20 in.

Plate 4

THE WEST HIGHLANDS, SOUND OF MULL   Oil 25 × 30 in.

Plate 5

THE DRAWING-ROOM, CROFT HOUSE   Oil $24\frac{1}{2} \times 29\frac{1}{2}$ in.

Plate 6

IONA FARM   Water-colour $6\frac{3}{4} \times 9\frac{3}{8}$ in.

Plate 7

THE BOXERS

Oil sketch 17½ × 14⅜ in.

THE BIPLANE

Pen and chalk 13⅛ × 10⅛ in.

Pen and chalk 13⅜ × 10⅝ in.

THE TWO JOCKS

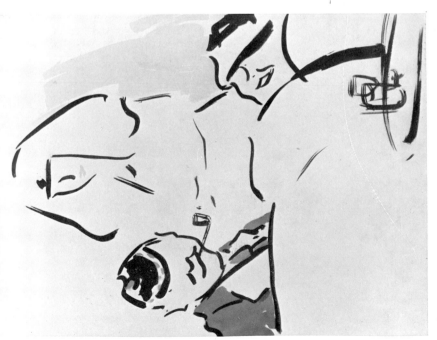

Pen and chalk 13⅜ × 10⅝ in.

IN HOSPITAL

Plate 8

Leslie Hunter

1879–1931

Leslie Hunter

Leslie Hunter

1879–1931

GEORGE LESLIE HUNTER was born in Rothesay, Scotland, in 1879. In his boyhood he was addressed as George, but in later years, except in the family circle, he was known as Leslie. Some earlier works bear the signature 'G. Leslie Hunter'; subsequently the G. was dropped and later on he was content to sign himself 'L. Hunter.' During the last period of residence at Saint Paul in the Alpes Maritimes, for some undiscoverable reason he was called 'Jimmy' by a small group of associates.

The foregoing is the first paragraph of a short biographical sketch which I was privileged to write many years ago. It may well stand, but I have gathered some more information since the book *Introducing Leslie Hunter* was published.

Hunter's father, William, was born in Carluke where his people were farmers. They had originally come from East Kilbride, and it was quite well known, in the family circle at any rate, that they were related to William and John Hunter, famous names in the history of medicine in Glasgow and London, whose names are commemorated in the Hunterian Museum at the University. The old mill where Hunter's grandfather lived and worked still stands, and there is a Hunter Street in the village of East Kilbride, which is now marked for development into one of Scotland's new towns.

William Hunter qualified as a dispensing chemist and engaged in that business in Rothesay for a number of years. All five of his family were born there and received their early education at Rothesay Academy.

On the maternal side Hunter's forbears were also of good

farming stock. His grandmother came from the south end of Kintyre, and after her marriage lived in Glasgow to the ripe age of ninety-two. Her husband, in his younger days, was in the Army and fought at Waterloo. His medal and discharge papers, signed by Wellington, are still in the possession of the family. This wonderful old lady was remembered by her grandchildren as a great reader with a marvellous memory and a fund of stories about Old Glasgow. Her daughter was born in Monteith Row and continued to live there until she married William Hunter, with whom she made their first home in Rothesay.

It is interesting to recall that another forbear of Hunter's was his father's uncle, Robert Forest, who was born in Carluke in 1790 and died in 1852. Forest appears to have been a very competent monumental sculptor, and a short sketch of his early career was published in 1832 by Robert Chambers of *Chambers's Journal*. The John Knox statue in Glasgow, designed by Warnes, and the Lord Melville statue in Edinburgh, designed by Chantrey (of the famous Chantrey Bequest), were executed by Forest. At one time the Calton Hill, Edinburgh, was decorated with several of his works. He was also responsible for the huge carved figure of William Wallace which occupies a prominent niche in the wall of the Parish Church in Lanark.

Some years ago I had a letter from the late Mr W. G. Hunter of California, an elder brother of Leslie. He told me about another member of the Forest family—a courageous lady who took up painting when sixty years of age. Evidently she was not without ability for she was commissioned to paint the portrait of a distinguished gentleman, but when the portrait was finished the patron was not at all pleased with the result. After some discussion the ' artist ' settled the matter by remarking, ' Ah weel ! I'll just put a beard on it and it'll dae for John Knox.' So much for hereditary influence.

Hunter's father was a man of wide interests, and was one

of the founders of the Physical and Archaeological Society of Bute, now the Bute Natural History Society. He was also a devout man. Family legend has it that Leslie gave early indications of the ' strange necessity ' by spending the hour of church attendance in making rapid sketches of the nodding heads of the worshippers.

Hunter's eldest brother was a medical student at Glasgow University. As he was about to sit for his final examinations he ' caught a chill ' which ended in his untimely death. A sister had died a short time previously, and this double tragedy had a devastating effect on a happy family circle. It led William Hunter to look for a change and there was no difficulty in persuading him to emigrate to California. He was influenced by some family friends who were in Rothesay for a visit, and who painted glowing pictures of the advantages and attraction waiting on the Pacific Coast.

Hunter's schooling at Rothesay Academy had been of the usual solid kind common to the Scottish Educational system. Emigration to America put an end to schooldays when he was thirteen, and for the next four years he was content to leave it at that. After a vain effort to make him a farmer he was allowed to develop his talents in the field of art. His earlier work was chiefly devoted to magazine and book illustration, but after a visit to Paris the urge to become a painter was irresistible.

For several years he was one of the distinguished Bohemian group of artists, poets and writers, which included Jack London, Will Irwin, who wrote a fascinating account of old San Francisco, Gelett Burgess, famous writer of nonsense verses, Robert Aitken, sculptor, Jacquin Miller, the poet, and many other artists and writers. Most of them had to fight a constant battle against privation and disappointments, but they ultimately triumphed. Years later Will Irwin wrote the foreword to the catalogue of an exhibition of paintings by Hunter in New York. He recalled the old days when they ' starved together.' Actually there was no need for

Hunter to starve. His family was behind him, then and always, but he kept faithful to the formula of independence which was the essential qualification in Bohemia.

Hunter's first one-man exhibition, although completely planned, was never opened. The San Francisco earthquake and fire in 1906 occurred on the day preceding this important event of his history and all his paintings were destroyed. There is, of course, no record of the nature of his work at this time.[1] He had exhibited very occasionally with the Californian Society of Artists—the Salon des Réfusés of San Francisco—but without any success. Whatever living he made from his art was derived from magazine illustration work. Some of these sketches are still in existence, but they reveal nothing more than ordinary competence. He contrived a visit to Paris, and this appears to have changed his entire outlook, for on his return he announced to his friends his intention of getting down to the serious business of painting.

The files of the *Sunset Magazine* for the years 1903–1906 and a *Railroad Monthly* of the same period show that he was occupied with fair regularity ; and for some years later, in spite of his high intentions, he returned now and again to the ' hack work ' which he affected to despise. All this time his industry in making sketches was enormous. Any scene, person or occasion was captured in a swiftly executed drawing, and he seemed to have had few other interests.

The Hunter family had returned to Scotland in 1910, not because the venture had failed but rather because Hunter's father had an overwhelming nostalgia for the homeland. He did not survive long to enjoy the peace and quiet of his homeland, for he died in Pitlochry that same year.

Leslie had been left behind in California, probably because of his self-sufficiency and confidence that he could

---

[1] In March 1950 at the Huntington Library, California, U.S.A., I was shown the *Overland Monthly* for September 1902, a memorial number to Bret Harte with some illustrations by Hunter. The San Francisco Directory of 1900 includes Hunter as designer and illustrator at 611 Clay Street.

make his way. Eventually he too returned to Scotland, where for a year, in spite of all his high intentions to get down to painting, he was compelled to continue with magazine and book illustration. He did some work for Collins, the well-known Glasgow publishers, and a few sketches appeared in the *Scots Pictorial* (now merged in the Glasgow *Bulletin*). Now and then, assailed by fresh hopes, he would dash to London and Paris. The *Pall Mall Magazine* and the *Graphic* commissioned some drawings, and he had one exciting trip to Berlin.

Although Hunter appears to have been afflicted with a fever of restlessness which compelled him to follow this or that gleam, after each new adventure he was always to be found in Glasgow. His mother's home was his permanent address. Hunter was very devoted to his mother. He had a great respect for her intelligence and courage, and the several sketches and a portrait in oils (1908), with his mother as the subject, show a remarkable family resemblance and reveal a Whistlerian influence in his early work. The death of his mother in 1913 affected him seriously. Her faith and encouragement had supported him through the bad patches, and although she left him enough money to keep financial anxiety at a distance for many years, it took him a long time to adapt himself to a completely new situation. A brother and sister still remained to form a family background. The former, William Hunter, continued in business in Glasgow until 1920 when he returned to California. His sister, Mrs Jeanie Macfarlane, gradually began to fill the mother's role, and it was to her home, 147 Crow Road, Glasgow, that, in times of depression, fatigue of mind or of body, he always returned.

In due course he became a well-known figure in Glasgow Art circles, was elected to membership of the Art Club, occupied a number of studios, many of which he fitted up with sleeping accommodation, but if he couldn't be found in his usual haunts, or had failed to leave an address when he went abroad, contact was always established through Mrs Macfarlane at Crow Road. His erratic mode of living must frequently have been rather a trial, but his sister left him to conduct his life as he wanted to, quite happy to be available if and when called upon.

There were often periods in Hunter's life when he appeared to be poverty-stricken. In San Francisco, London, Paris and Glasgow his friends were often distressed at the signs of poverty. There was actually no need for this, because his family, without qualifications, had made it clear that he could always turn in their direction. Quite often, especially after a successful exhibition, the substantial proceeds seemed to disappear with remarkable speed. He would indulge in an orgy of buying frames, canvases and paints, etc., and forget all about the ' nest-egg ' that still remained. Throughout his life he had little regard for money as such. Cheques were frequently mislaid, and then when a rent payment was due or money was required urgently, instead of considering his financial state or recollecting what had happened to the last credit balance he decided that the only thing which would meet the situation was to sell a picture. And if pictures were not selling he would just have to try to get along somehow until they did. It was all rather extraordinary and not easy to explain, but in the light of fuller knowledge we can only look upon it as a minor eccentricity.

His carelessness in money affairs was equalled by his almost complete disregard of fashion in the matter of personal dress and appearance. In later years when he began to put on weight his jacket buttons always seemed to be on the point of breaking adrift, and the general untidiness of his clothing certainly made it easy to assume that he was on intimate terms with adversity. There was nothing bizarre in his dress. He was just generally shabby. If his attention was drawn to a hole in the heel of a sock, he would camouflage the gap with some paint until it was convenient to effect repairs.

Plate I

CHRYSANTHEMUMS   Oil 27 × 22½ in.

Hunter was never a poseur. He was unconscious of disorder. He had one consuming passion—his art. Nothing else really mattered. Certainly, if it was required of him, he entered into the spirit of an occasion, sometimes rather slowly, but if he did not become bored because of its inadequacy, he warmed up with enthusiasm and zest. And he could dress up for a party, especially if some amateur valet was at hand.

It was shortly before the First World War (1914–18) that Hunter's work was brought to the notice of Alexander Reid. Up till then he had found an odd patron for a still life or flower painting. One of his patrons, a church friend of his mother, had commissioned a large still-life in which Hunter was required to incorporate some family treasures and harmonise the whole with the dining-room scheme of decoration. This amazing composition created considerable interest and was seen by a number of people, among whom were several who ultimately claimed that they had ' discovered ' a young artist of such promise as to justify calling Reid's attention to his work. In any event, Reid's interest was aroused. He bought one or two paintings, gave some wise counsel, and promised an exhibition when a sufficient number of new projects was completed. Greatly encouraged by this Hunter went to France, perhaps in search of ideas, solitude, paintable places, warmth or colour.

In August 1914 he was in Etaples when his sketching excursions led the excited authorities to look upon him with suspicion. His fresh complexion and fair hair were enough evidence for the spy maniacs in search of Teutonic agents and he was arrested. However, the machinery of the law did not seem to have been very effective, for he managed to escape in the direction of Paris. The war excitement in Paris was of course intense, and Hunter was bewildered. An account of his experiences which came at first-hand from E. A. Taylor of Kirkcudbright has already appeared [1]

[1] Honeyman, *Introducing Leslie Hunter* (1937)

and need not here be elaborated. It is enough to say that he returned to Scotland, was excused army service on a variety of grounds, and throughout most of the war years worked on an uncle's farm at Millburn in Lanarkshire. There he did all that was required of him to the complete satisfaction of men and animals. He also found time to paint several fine pictures. Many of these were made from early sketches, but the best of them were still-lifes and interiors of the farm kitchen. A typical example of this period is now in the Tate Gallery.

The promised exhibition was held in 1916. It was his first important exhibition in this country, and on the whole it was very successful. The Glasgow *Bailie* (now defunct) summed up the case in one or two illuminating sentences : ' Leslie Hunter is not likely to be a martyr in a town like Glasgow, which has been fond of breaking old conventions, but he has made certain affirmations in paint that will be disputed by those who do not get right into his atmosphere. . . . We have to respect Leslie Hunter, as we respect the strong man who is cutting a path for us and leading us through the forest.' With this blessing and the financial results he could afford to ignore the adverse or lukewarm notices, and for the next few years he concentrated on ' improving his technique.' He also appears to have made a valiant effort towards a more systematic and disciplined way of living, and with this end in view read or consulted the writings of a wide range of artist-critics and men of letters.

On the first two pages of a notebook which he used at this time there are some neat entries of current receipts and payments. But the adventure into accountancy was quickly abandoned, and the remaining leaves are scribbled with an interesting variety of *obiter dicta* (the sources of some are noted). Here are a few : ' Energy, freshness and masterly disposition, the three elements that mark the classic.' ' When I sit down to make a sketch from nature I try to forget I have ever seen a picture—Constable.' ' Punctuality. Personal

Attention. Courage. Thoroughness. Genius is nothing but diligence and labour. *Hogarth.*' Hunter forgot all these except courage. One underlined entry—which he certainly adhered to—runs thus, ' Everyone must choose his own way and mine will be the way of colour.'

In this valuable notebook are long extracts from articles about Cézanne, Van Gogh and Gauguin. Some of them relate to the controversies which surrounded the first Post-impressionist exhibition in London (1910). But it should be remembered that Hunter's first visit to Paris was in 1904. This is known through Mr S. S. White of Philadelphia who recollected the young Scots artist—ill-clad, under-nourished, restlessly active. From him Mr White had purchased a few drawings, partly because he was amazed at the rapidity with which they had been done and partly as a gesture of encouragement. It is therefore more than likely that Hunter was well aware of the ferment of Post-impressionism and the emergence of ' Les Fauves.' In any case he had made careful notes of the colours that each of the great figures, Cézanne, Van Gogh and Gauguin, had arranged on their palettes. Moreover, he had sketched completely the palettes, outdoor and indoor, of McTaggart and Whistler. Beneath his outline of Whistler's palette Hunter has written, ' The palette from first to last should be orderly, measured, rational,' and this, ' The palette is the instrument on which the painter plays his harmony. It must be beautiful always as the tenderly-cared-for violin of the great musician is kept in condition worthy of his music.' This counsel of perfection probably comes from Whistler, but although Hunter has filled three more pages with similar observations, it would be placing an undue strain on the imagination to describe him as a faithful disciple. When his own palette became heavy with the incrustations of dried paint he preferred to start a new one. Those discarded would be restored to use in the general tidying-up processes of removal to a new studio.

During the immediate post-war years Hunter found plenty

to do and his circle of friends increased. Most of them had come to know him through his paintings. The introductions were generally made by Reid whose gallery was a port of call to old and new collectors. In Glasgow particularly the late William McInnes, William McNair and Ion Harrison, associates in a prominent shipping firm, formed a trio which was in more or less constant touch with Hunter till the day of his death. McInnes, who died in 1944, bequeathed his fine collection of pictures to the city of Glasgow. Among superb examples by Degas, Monet, Seurat, Cézanne, Matisse, Braque and many others there is a group of fine and varied paintings by Hunter, and five Peploes.

In Dundee the late John Tattersall and the late Matthew Justice were staunch friends who, in addition to their generous hospitality when Hunter visited the town, did much to create interest and make new clients. Justice maintained an irregular correspondence with Hunter for many years, and it is chiefly through this that the history of the final decade of the artist's life has been preserved. The quality of the Hunter-Justice friendship may be gleaned from a letter received by the writer from Matthew Justice shortly before his death : '. . . dear lovable Leslie Hunter. One time he came to stay with me for a weekend and stayed three weeks. The day before he left he sent a note to his sister saying he had arrived. I went down to the Tay Bridge Station to see him off to Glasgow. He was seated in the last compartment of the train. After waiting about a quarter of an hour I asked Hunter when the train was timed to leave (I was sitting in the carriage along with him). He said he didn't know. When I went out to the platform I found the train had gone, the carriage Hunter was sitting in had not been attached to the train. He came back with me to the warehouse, and in the evening to my house where he stayed for another week.'

In 1922 Hunter had a long tour on the Continent—Paris, Venice, Florence and one or two places along the Riviera coast. He saw a good deal of J. D. Fergusson, and in view

Plate II

THE STORM, LARGO   Oil 16 × 20 in.

Plate III

THE MALACCA CANE (Portrait of Duncan Macdonald Esq)   Oil 30 × 25 in.

of J. D.'s subsequent decision to return to Scotland, where he had been for the last ten years, it is interesting to note what Hunter wrote in 1922. ' We [Fergusson, Peploe and Hunter] propose, if possible, some lectures in Glasgow on modern art to colour this winter—Fry, if one can get him, etc. . . . Fergusson proposes that Scotland takes its place as foremost in culture as in war. I've felt that the taste is here if they only get the chance. What a necessary adjunct art and beauty is to life ! I believe this feeling is in the race, only submerged.'

There was the London exhibition of works by Peploe, Cadell and Hunter at the Leicester Galleries, arranged through McNeill Reid in 1923, and while it was on the whole well received Hunter was not satisfied. He appeared to be unduly sensitive to the criticism, and laboured under the conviction that his work was not wholly satisfactory. It was at this time that he had the first of his recurrent ' nervous breakdowns.' He recovered quickly, and spent some time in Fife where he was frequently visited by his friends from Dundee and Glasgow. And he was in excellent painting form. His Fife landscapes at this period were greatly admired and won for him fresh support, as the subsequent exhibitions in Glasgow and Edinburgh unmistakably proved. The sales were perhaps not so numerous in Edinburgh, but his reputation was more firmly established. Guided by the friends whom he had consulted he made a joint agreement with Reid's and Aitken Dott, whereby these firms would have the first call on his output in return for a minimum guarantee of £600 per annum. This freed him from any financial anxieties for the next few years.

He made a quick visit to America but did not proceed beyond New York, and seemed to have had an attack of home-sickness. A postcard records, ' I am tired of seeing things and people, though it has been a change to rest. Am now anxious to get back to Fife and get some work done. Met Augustus John here.'

In June 1924 the modern Scottish movement was represented by Cadell, Fergusson, Hunter and Peploe at the Galerie Barbazanges in Paris. This was the first time any substantial number of Hunter's pictures (seventeen) had been shown in Paris, and one critic at least thought highly of them. He wrote, ' Like all modernists who have followed Cézanne, Hunter has profited by the great lesson given by the illustrious Provençal and has applied the construction to his own proper development, for he is not, in any sense, an imitator of the Master.' It is interesting to compare that with *The Scotsman's* critic in 1948 (see page 11), and it is equally interesting to note the further observation of the anonymous French critic :

It must not be forgotten that Hunter does not paint for the present but for the future. In time his pictures will acquire an invaluable patina, and it would appear that prudence counsels him to prefer the approval of the future to a passing renown.

For the next three years Hunter worked mainly in Scotland. He painted landscape in Fife, had one happy interval among the houseboats in Loch Lomond, and produced an irregular flow of flowers and still-life pictures. He was not by any means prolific, for he had spells when his work failed to please him. He was rather careless with his unfinished canvases, either giving them away or leaving them behind when he changed quarters. Their reappearance in recent years has been a disservice to his memory. The Loch Lomond pictures of this period, when compared with those he did six years later, probably help to establish more than other comparisons the frequent changes in approach and technique which is so apparent in his later and more personal productions.

In January 1925 there was a second Scottish group show at the Leicester Gallery—Peploe, Hunter, Cadell and Fergusson. W. R. Sickert wrote an entertaining preface to the catalogue. The exhibition served to establish more firmly the London reputations of Peploe and Fergusson. The notices favoured them, and although some were very appreciative of Hunter's ten pictures these were not submitted to any real criticism.

Although his paintings were selling well in Scotland, and plans for future exhibitions in Dundee, Edinburgh and Glasgow were in the making, Hunter became very unsettled. He thought his work was losing vitality ; that quality which he constantly asserted was the one thing which must never be sacrificed. In the Glasgow Art Club his views on art generally were looked upon as somewhat fantastic and he himself ' a bit queer.' His artist neighbours in the West George Street studio would report frequent noisy altercations going on in Hunter's studio, and on investigation they would find that Hunter was alone. The only objective symptom of the neurosis which afflicted him for the remainder of his life was this habit of vehement argument with some unknown and always absent antagonist. His peace of mind was disturbed. He regretted the time ' wasted in the studio " landscaping." ' ' I feel after the New Year I will have to make up for it before I'll have peace of mind and feel sociable. I've been working under a nervous strain, and a neuralgia attack has given me little sleep in three weeks.'

Every now and then the pull southwards would grow stronger, and the old arguments against his going would be resumed by the friends who thought his career would suffer. They felt it would be a case of ' out of sight out of mind.'

Eventually he made the break, and from 1927 to 1929 he was in the south of France. Letters indicate that he moved from place to place, but his favourite spot was Saint-Paul. He claimed, in reply to a query regarding his activities, that he knew the Mediterranean Coast from Monte Carlo to Cassis and had made a hundred drawings of various places. McNeill Reid and Duncan Macdonald kept asking for pictures. They wanted to keep his work on view and were arranging for an exhibition in London. They had reserved the month of May 1928 ; but Hunter kept on postponing the day. He quoted Peploe, who was at Cassis, in support of his scheme of making innumerable drawings as the best preparation for learning to know the country, and that very soon he would feel like painting the ' spirit ' of it. All that summer he worked with great energy, writing to say that he was painting in fine style and that his friends in and around Saint-Paul were greatly impressed. The exhibition took place in October. It was not very successful. The critics thought it was stimulating enough, but on the whole not very satisfying. They wanted ' the reticence which betokens thought and gives permanent significance to art.' Oddly enough Hunter was not upset over the lukewarm reception given to his first independent show in London. He seemed to have regained confidence in himself. He was convinced that in design, colour and the essential vitality his art had developed a maturity and a purpose lacking in his earlier efforts. It was a pity that sales were less frequent, but so long as he felt this new power within him the business side of the affair would have to take care of itself a bit longer. So he returned to Saint-Paul and continued to paint in what he called ' a thin fashion,' because he saw this as ' the way to get the luminous quality of the country.'

Early in 1929 he was in New York, urged to go there by J. D. Fergusson and John Ressich, who thought that Hunter would be more likely to find there a public for his ' advanced ' type of picture. He greatly enjoyed this trip, partly because his exhibition in the Ferargil Galleries brought him considerable notice in a wide range of newspapers and magazines. Moreover, these notices seemed to reveal a greater understanding of what he was attempting to do. Will Irwin, the friend of San Francisco days, who had by then become famous in American journalism, wrote a sparkling foreword to the catalogue, and the New York *Times* reproduced one of his pictures. The critic of this leading American journal wrote: ' Mr Hunter's strongest point is his colour, which is gay and attractive attaining a luscious brilliancy . . . he is one of those artists in whom style and spontaneity play a

Oil $21\frac{1}{2} \times 25\frac{1}{2}$ in.

large part.' The Brooklyn *Daily Times* went further: ' There is nothing half-hearted or theoretically lugubrious about his work. It sets forth the " healthy and personal reaction with a casualness that almost conceals its art. It repudiates formalism and yet it is aesthetically sound and real. Above all, it is individual and personal.'

The exhibition did not bring immediate financial results of an exciting character, but other dealers became interested, and he was rather elated to find that in New York the prices put on his work were nearly four times higher than those which had been asked in Glasgow or London.

The social round in New York soon began to pall. He was anxious to return to Saint-Paul. Suggestions that he should go home to Glasgow were brushed aside. He had heard that some friends there did not look with a kindly eye on his more recent work, and this may have led him to write to his cousin, Arthur Leyden, ' I detest Glasgow. I met a lot of Americans in the south of France and like much more to be in their company.'

The summer of 1929 found him again on the Riviera feeling in very good health and spirits and beginning to get some amusement out of life. On his way along the coast to Saint-Paul he halted for a few days at places such as Cassis and Saint-Tropez. Unfortunately his state of well-being did not last long. McInnes, who had met him in the course of a holiday visit to the Mediterranean, reported on his return to Glasgow in September that he had been shocked by Hunter's appearance. They had dined together at Toulon, and Hunter was looking miserably thin and unhappy. He was *distrait* in manner and seemed to find it difficult to sustain conversation on any topic, breaking off into irrelevant observations. As it turned out these were the premonitory symptoms of his most serious breakdown in health.

After his meeting with McInnes he had returned to his studio in Saint-Paul, and his friends there, notably Joan Smith, who ran the ' English Tea-Room,' were equally

shocked at the change in him. He began to shut himself
up in his studio, always working, entirely regardless of his
personal comfort. His old obsession returned, and noisy
altercations with his ' enemy' became the common gossip
and concern of the village. Not that anyone, man, woman
or child, was afraid of him; he was much too gentle and
kindly in the lucid moments, especially when he attended
meals at the Colombe d'Or or at Joan Smith's place; meals
to which he had to be unceremoniously summoned. The
climax was reached when he became acutely ill. He had
accidentally taken some turpentine mixture in mistake for
some wine which was in a similar bottle. It had not at
first upset him, but the appearance of disquieting symptoms
compelled his removal to a hospital at Nice.

Fortunately Hunter's powers of physical recovery were
excellent. His sister, Mrs Macfarlane, brought him home
to Glasgow, and her care and attention soon brought about
the restoration of a sadly debilitated body. The mental
depression did not lift quite so quickly. This breakdown
was much more severe than any previous one, and while
the enforced idleness was irksome he was harassed with
doubts and a sense of desolation, because so few of his friends
seemed to appreciate the only kind of picture he felt any
urge to paint. The few friends, however, supplied the
necessary encouragement, for very shortly he began to
produce some of his finest works and acquired a confidence
which no amount of adverse comment could shake.

At first it was by no means plain sailing. The chief
difficulty was that of finance. He had not sold a picture for
a long time, and the world-wide slump coincided with his
resumption of work. The joint-agreement with Reid and
Aitken Dott had terminated two years before and a con-
tinuance was certainly not a business proposition. However,
everybody concerned recognised that until better times
returned the only thing to do was to adopt a make-shift
policy. Hunter would paint pictures, and Reid's, chiefly

through organising a band of friends, would see to it that
sales were enough to keep things going. It has to be remembered that at this time the citizens of Glasgow, as elsewhere,
had quite a sufficiency of anxieties, and that picture-collect-
ing had anything but a high place. Nevertheless there
was plenty of fun and excitement, and Hunter played a
prominent part in the pleasures—visual and mental—of a
number of friends who enjoyed his company and who were
convinced that the lamp of his genius remained undimmed.

The custom of morning coffee which was a feature of
Glasgow business life helped to establish an almost daily
contact with Hunter. He was enjoying life, although his
absent-mindedness and the frequent flare-up of his neurosis
caused occasional anxiety. If he failed to turn up at the
usual meeting-place someone would investigate, interrupt
his work if need be, and see to it that he did not forget that
food was a necessity. Any regular mode of life was beyond
his power to establish, but if things appeared to be getting
out of hand his sister invariably came to the rescue and a
spell in her home worked wonders in the way of restoration.
And in the interval his studio would receive a thorough
spring-cleaning.

A sketch-book was seldom out of his hand. The morning
coffee discussion which ranged from current topics to personalities and theories on art was more often centred on the
particular tasks then occupying Hunter's time and attention.
Before long out would come the sketch-book and pen, pencil
or crayons. One of his pockets would contain a mixed bunch
of these. He would illustrate the project of a picture or make
a rapid drawing of some attractive head at an adjoining
table.

This constant compulsion to express pictorially what was
in his mind was sometimes disconcerting. On one occasion,
at a house dinner in the Art Club, Hunter was a source of
considerable annoyance, tinged with amusement, to a very
busy staff. Whenever a fresh plate was placed before him to

await the next course he would produce a large fountain-pen, and in a moment or two the plate would be covered with an imaginative design or by a caricature of some nearby personality. Dr O. H. Mavor—now widely known as James Bridie—passed a menu card to him and challenged him to do one of me. The result was not very brilliant, and O. H. promptly did a better one on the other side. This is not surprising for O. H. has a peculiar talent for that sort of thing. His ' doodling ' is in its way as fascinating as his playwriting.

It is not so easy to recall how Hunter came to adventure into the field of portraiture. The idea may have germinated in the course of informal criticisms on the standards of portraiture in the usual annual exhibitions. He certainly used to argue that a spell of painting portraits would be a relief from flowers and still-lifes and that he was eager to demonstrate his fundamental conception of art to the effect that treatment, not subject, was the essential element in making pictures.

This was all very well, but in the absence of any reputation as a portrait painter the likelihood of commissions was remote. Once again the immediate circle of friends went into conference and emerged with a list of sitters who had been cajoled or coerced into taking part in the adventure. This is not the place to give a catalogue of names, but it may be assumed that it required some faith in the artist's sincerity and capacity to induce the sitters to devote the time and to bear with his unpunctual habits and the discomforts of his studio. With one or two he failed completely. He was anxious to do Ion Harrison in his kilt and sketched out two full length portraits which were to make Raeburn's *The McNab* look like the work of an amateur. He laboured at the canvas for quite a time, but in the end it was abandoned as a failure. In some cases the sitters or their friends were not very impressed with the final results—some have since changed their minds—but one or two of the portraits Hunter

Plate V

HOUSE BOATS, BALLOCH   Oil 20 × 24 in.

did at this time hold their place among the important productions of his career. Mention must be made of that grand old man of the British Theatre, Charles B. Cochran (now Sir Charles). He was in Glasgow for several weeks rehearsing *Evergreen*, and because of his lifelong interest in art we had many happy meetings inspecting great paintings in public and private collections. He agreed to become one of Hunter's victims, and for days on end the artist haunted the King's Theatre. He did innumerable sketches of scenes in the show and worked at a large portrait of C. B. with the King's Theatre stage as a background. It was, of course, impossible to get more than fleeting views of the main subject, but the picture was eventually completed in time for inclusion in the Paris Exhibition. This exhibition, as has been recorded elsewhere, was a great success. Hunter was thrilled by it. His visit to Paris and the renewal of old friendships there and in London led him to arrive at certain well-defined conclusions. The first of these was that Glasgow was finished —at any rate for the present—as a centre of art appreciation. Prospects in London was infinitely brighter. He proposed looking for a studio there and to continue to paint portraits. And something entirely new for him was contemplated. He intended to do a series of pictures of London scenes. He had come to the conclusion that Whistler and all the others had failed to give any idea of its marvellous colour. He had thoughts of a new technique which would enable him to capture the essence of it, but first of all he had decided to spend the summer finishing off the work he had started at Loch Lomond.

The final stages in Hunter's career were notable for the paintings he did on Loch Lomondside and for the drawings he did of Hyde Park. These latter were to be the prelude to a larger plan, and they occupied him for several weeks between visits to Glasgow from which the Reid firm also was now in process of transferring to London. The Lefevre Gallery was his London headquarters, and he was in constant touch with Reid and Macdonald. He was often at the latter's flat in the evenings or at weekends, and there plans for the future were shaped into more definite form. Reid recollects that Hunter seemed completely to have regained his old fervour, not only as it affected his work, but also in his talks on art affairs in general. He revisited the national collections and looked in at the dealers to see what was happening in contemporary art. To visit an exhibition with him was always a refreshing and valuable experience. He had the great gift of being able to understand, almost at first glance, exactly what the painter's purpose was, and he would discuss the result from that starting-point. If he were moved into making an adverse comment on a particular passage he would qualify it by insisting that the final assessment could only be determined on the total statement attempted by the artist and not on an isolated phrase.

In the midst of all this activity in London, Hunter's friends became alarmed at indications that he was far from well. He dismissed the symptoms as ' indigestion,' and tried to find relief in ' stomach powders ' and such-like nostrums. But the discomfort persisted, sometimes to the accompaniment of acute, agonising pain. He was at last persuaded to return to Glasgow, and firmly advised to have a thorough medical overhaul.

On the day of his return he was in a cheerful mood and took pleasure in showing the London drawings to his intimate friends. He told them that everything was arranged for a fresh venture. The studio in London had been fixed. In the meantime he simply must paint a study of some wonderful flowers with which somebody had welcomed him home. He spent the entire day of his arrival painting in his studio. Late at night he arrived exhausted and in great pain at his sister's home, and eventually he was taken to a nursing home. An urgent operation revealed a condition beyond remedy and he died shortly afterwards. Contentment of mind and freedom from pain were the accompaniments of his passing, but the unfulfilled promise of his high hopes and aspirations seemed to his friends to be the supreme tragedy of his life.

To Hunter life and art were the same. He faced both with confidence, without thought of the consequences which might follow a determined course of action so long as that course was taken with honesty of purpose. At the end he was sustained by the knowledge that his efforts had become appreciated not only at home but abroad. The growth in that appreciation has not been swift, but up till now it has been sure.

I opened this account with a passage from a fuller biography which appeared in 1937. It seems appropriate to conclude by repeating the closing passages which have perhaps become a fulfilled prophecy :

When you read the story of his life in the light of his work it will not be difficult to give a name to his pictures. You will not ask to see ' a painting by Leslie Hunter '—you simply say, ' a Leslie Hunter ' —some day it may be ' a Hunter.' There is really nothing abstruse or intricate about this, for it is the formula for all art worthy of survival.

Art, of all created things, is greater than its maker. It becomes a separate thing. And however much you may discount my enthusiasm and whatever be the final appraisal, I hold this as proved : Leslie Hunter denied himself many of the ordinary comforts of life for the sake of his art. It was first always. His reward is that it has outlived him, claiming his name for its own, acquiring his personality and speaking his language.

Plate 1

FIFE VILLAGE   Oil 21½ × 18 in.

Plate 2

BOATS, LOCH LOMOND   Oil 21½ × 26½ in.

Plate 3

ROSES IN GLASS VASE   Oil 25 × 20 in.

Plate 4

LOBSTER ON BLUE PLATE   Oil 14 × 16 in.

Plate 5

INTERIOR WITH FIGURE   Oil 22 × 18 in.

Plate 6

THE HARBOUR, VILLEFRANCHE　　　　　　　Oil 18 × 22 in.

Plate 7

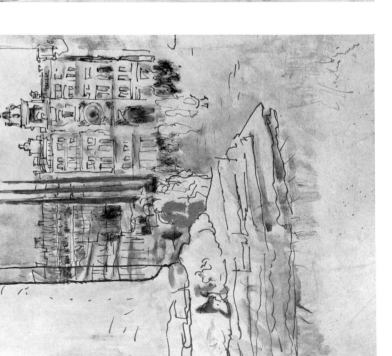

INTERIOR OF FRENCH CHURCH Water-colour 20½ × 16 in.

THE CLOCK TOWER, VENICE   Water-colour 12½ × 9½ in.

Plate 8

FIFE COTTAGE   Water-colour 20 × 24 in.

ROTTEN ROW,   HYDE PARK, LONDON   Pen and chalk 16 × 21½ in.

As I Remember Them

by

Ion R. Harrison

As I Remember Them

by ION R. HARRISON

IT was in 1921 or 1922 that I first became interested in the work of the three Scottish Colourists. The first exhibition of Peploe's which I saw was in Alex. Reid & Lefevre's, West George Street, Glasgow. Mr Peploe at that time had an Exhibition of Flower Pictures, mostly, so far as I remember, of tulips—red, yellow and white—painted against blue backgrounds with different coloured draperies. I had never seen anything in art similar to these pictures, and I did not understand them. They really startled me for, to my eyes, they were so 'ultra-modern.' The formal manner in which the tulips were painted, and their brilliant colour against equally strong draperies, were at that time beyond my comprehension. A Tulip picture of this phase of Peploe's work is one of his pictures which I now cherish most highly.

The first pictures I bought of the three Scottish Colourists were from a Peploe exhibition at Reid's which was held in March 1924. One was the beautiful *Pink Rose* Picture, Plate VI, and the other the smaller storm seascape painted at the North End, Iona. I recollect the thrill it gave me to hang my first two Peploe's, and how disappointed I was when the majority of my friends did not appreciate them.

I well remember buying my first Leslie Hunter, also at a one-man exhibition of Hunter's, at Reid's about 1925. It was the upright picture of the Cottages in Fife and was the highest-priced picture in the exhibition, viz £48. When leaving, old Mr Alex. Reid said to me that if he was a wealthy man he would buy every Hunter in the exhibition. I naturally took this to be a bit of dealer's blarney, for after all Mr Reid's business was to sell pictures—not to buy them. However, if Mr Reid had done so he would have made a very fine investment.

The first Cadell I bought would be soon after buying the Hunter Fifeshire Landscape. It is known as the *Pink Azalea*. I recall that when Cadell first visited Croft House in 1928 he saw, on entering the front door, the *Pink Azalea* hanging on the wall in a room to his left. He went straight up to it and, sucking his pipe, looked at it silently for some time. Eventually he turned towards me and said, ' I have often wondered where that picture went. I congratulate you on having acquired it and, although I say it myself, you have a d——d good Cadell,' and broke into his infectious laugh. Such were the beginnings of my Peploe, Hunter, Cadell Collection which, including oils, water-colours, crayons and drawings, now number over 170 examples, covering what Cadell used to call a ' cradle to the grave collection.'

Occasionally I have visitors who take a special interest in the work of these three artists. Almost invariably, before they leave the house, they ask me whom I consider to be the greatest artist of the three. My reply is that I consider them all to be equally great, each in his own special way. One of them could excel in painting something which another could not tackle quite so successfully. For instance, Cadell certainly excelled in painting interiors in a manner which neither Peploe nor Hunter could equal. I also think that Cadell was the most versatile of the three. He painted landscapes, seascapes, figure subjects, cows, sheep, ships and boats with equal facility. One of the finest pictures of a horse race I have ever seen was a small oil painted by Cadell. To my mind it equalled for action, both of horses and jockeys, anything ever painted by Degas. It was on view at a small sale Cadell had in his house when he lived in Regent Terrace, Edinburgh. Unfortunately for me, it had been sold just an hour before I arrived. I told Cadell that I was willing to give double the price for it if the purchaser would sell it back again, but he refused to do so. Cadell told me that this was the one and only occasion on which he had ever painted a horse race.

As a generalisation I call Peploe the Blue Painter, Cadell the Green Painter and Hunter the Red Painter, for there are very few pictures by any of these artists which do not show a distinct trace of their fondness for their own particular colour. After I got to know Cadell he lived in three different houses in Edinburgh, and in each one of them he painted the doors and windows green, as also he did his cottage in Iona. It became a matter of habit to talk about 'Cadell Green.' Although these three artists had their individualistic style of painting, yet they all hang in a room side by side harmoniously. With the exception of their very early works, when they used black backgrounds, their more mature and later pictures are all painted in a high key, and so they blend together in happy unison.

Leslie Hunter was the first of the three whom I got to know personally. He was already a friend of my two partners, the late Mr Wm McInnes and Mr Wm McNair, and I must have met Hunter through them when I returned to business (after the 1914–18 War) in the autumn of 1919. He was a frequent visitor to the office when he was in Glasgow. He stayed twice with me for a night at Croft House, once in 1926 with Mr McInnes and again after my marriage. I note on referring to our visitors' book that his last visit was on the 30th April 1931, when he was also accompanied by Mr McInnes. My wife, who came from Florence, led us to talk a great deal about Italy, and Hunter told of his experiences in Venice and the south of France.

Cadell was the second whose acquaintance I made, some time later. I was spending a weekend in Edinburgh in the spring of 1928 and called on him at his house in Ainslie Place. He had just been removing from the ground floor to the second floor and had not yet fully settled in, but in spite of this he gave me a most kindly reception and instructed

Charles to show me his latest paintings. We seemed to take to each other immediately, and when I left he promised that the next time he was in the West he would visit us at Croft House, which promise he duly fulfilled. From then onwards he was a frequent visitor—sometimes staying for two or three weeks on end. At other times, if he was staying at Cove with the late Mr George Service he would come into the house unannounced and spend the day quite happily. On the other hand, whenever I was in Edinburgh I always made a point of going to see him, and we would spend the day visiting the Art Exhibitions on show at the R.S.A. or at the various dealers. We also spent a few happy days in Iona with Cadell in June 1932.

He served in the 'Dandy Ninth' as a private for nearly three years in the 1914 War, and in spite of his Colonel's remonstrances at his remaining a private he refused to take a commission, as he did not want to leave the small band of friends with whom he had joined the regiment. His C.O. pointed out to Cadell that he was shirking responsibility by not taking a commission. At last he reluctantly consented and was commissioned in the Argyll and Sutherland Highlanders. When he was still a private he was on leave for a few days in London. There he met one of his friends who had joined up with him in the 9th Royal Scots and who asked him to dine with him that night. Cadell said he regretted he could not as he had a previous engagement. His friend somewhat sarcastically said, 'Oh, I presume you are dining with a duke,' to which Cadell replied, 'On the contrary I am dining with two dukes.' This was the case, as he was the guest of his relative the Duke of Argyll who was accompanied by the Duke of Northumberland, and they dined at one of the fashionable clubs in the West End of London. Cadell said it was amusing to see the uplifted eyebrows of the other members of the club when they saw a private wearing a very war-stained kilt going into dinner.

If one had a party of friends Cadell was always the centre

of an animated group with his great fund of humour and his innumerable stories. He was a prince of entertainers, but he never required to be entertained himself. He and I seemed to have had a natural affinity in thought. He always regarded Peploe, who was so different in temperament to himself, as one of his closest friends and the finest artist that Scotland had produced, and both Cadell and Peploe shared a genuine admiration for Leslie Hunter's work.

It was through Cadell that I first met Peploe, and it was when Cadell was starting to paint a portrait of my wife that Peploe joined us at Croft House for a weekend. This was a very great privilege for us, for Peploe did not care for visiting people unless he knew them very well. It was a very happy weekend indeed, and Peploe was pleased to see his pictures hanging together in their surroundings. I told them how much they had helped me when I had come through some unhappy times. On the Sunday evening we visited the late Sir William Raeburn at Woodend, Helensburgh, and spent a very entertaining time with the old gentleman seeing his collection of pictures which included both Peploes and Cadells. Two or three years later we invited Mr and Mrs Peploe to come through to the private view of the Glasgow Art Institute and they accepted our invitation. Peploe told me that it was the first private view that he had ever been at in his life, a fact which astonished me. Because of his retiring and shy nature he avoided these occasions like the plague. We, therefore, felt it was a very great compliment to us that he had broken his rule. It was at this Institute that I bought a Peploe Flower and Fruit Picture with an abstract background. It was a type of Peploe which I had never seen before. Peploe told me that it had hung in his eldest son's room when the boy was at Oxford. I told Peploe that I was going to call the picture ' My Pepcasso,' a remark which, to my relief, greatly amused him.

I knew Peploe least of the three, but I held him in great esteem and regarded him as a very great artist. I had the sad privilege of attending his funeral with Cadell who waited for me to arrive from Glasgow. Cadell was frightfully nervous and very upset at the loss of his great friend. It was almost as if he had a foreboding that he himself had not long to live. At the graveside Cadell was so distressed that he had to walk away from the mourners. He just could not bear it. When we left the cemetery we went to tea with his cousin, Miss Wood, to whom he was much devoted. The composure of the old lady and the quiet of her charming drawing-room soothed Cadell's nerves, and when I left him to return home he was more his cheerful self again.

I often saw Hunter and Cadell paint, but I never saw Peploe at work, and I expect few ever did. He would be much too wrapped in thought to wish to have the intrusion of strangers while he was working. Hunter and Cadell both painted quickly and easily. The contrast in their palettes was indicative of their different personalities. Hunter's palette was invariably caked with huge lumps of paint of diverse colours, on the top of which he spilled turpentine which he splashed liberally over his suit, his feet and the floor. One wondered how he ever obtained any distinct colour out of such a conglomerate mess. His palette always reminded me of the Bass Rock or Ailsa Craig. On the other hand, Cadell was most meticulous in the keeping of his palette. At the end of his day's work he scraped every piece of paint off with his knife. He would then wash it thoroughly, and having dried it would burnish it and hang it up so that one could almost see one's face as in a mirror.

The contrast in their palettes applied equally to their clothes. Hunter was generally untidy and even unkempt in appearance. He often forgot when it was time to have his hair cut, and I think sometimes forgot that he had not shaved. Cadell in sharp contrast was always extremely well turned-out, and even although his clothes might be old they were always pressed and cleaned, and he always looked what he was—a gentleman. He was very fond of his kilt of Campbell tartan. It was given to him by the Duke of Argyll and had belonged to a previous ancestor of the Duke's family. Cadell claimed that his kilt was at least a hundred years old. Old and faded though it was it looked just right. With his kilt he usually wore a tweed jacket with a loud check which on most people would have looked ostentatious, but nevertheless seemed to blend with his flamboyant personality. Bunty claimed that nobody would ever guess that he was an artist by profession, nor indeed would they guess it from his personality. Nevertheless the artistic element was there, although I believe he was unconscious of it himself. He never painted during the winter—that is to say from the end of September until the middle of March, as he asserted that no-one could paint with any real sense of colour during the winter months in Scotland. For this reason in *Who's Who* he described his recreations as ' Bed and Billiards.'

Although Cadell's distinguished sister, Miss Jean Cadell, is a prominent actress Bunty had little liking for the theatre and seldom went to it. When he was staying at Croft House I once took him to see Sir John Martin Harvey who was acting in two plays on the same evening in the King's Theatre, the second one being ' The Bells.' It had been bequeathed to Sir John by H. B. Irving, who had received it from his father, Sir Henry Irving. Bunty consented to come to the theatre on this occasion, because he knew Sir John who had often stayed with the Cadells in bygone days when he was appearing in Edinburgh. After the performance we went round to the stage door and asked to see Sir John and were immediately admitted to his dressing-room. He greeted Bunty most warmly and asked many questions about Miss Jean Cadell, and how she was getting on. What struck me was that Martin Harvey was just the same off the stage as he was on. He still seemed to be acting. This I do not think was a pose, but was innate in an actor of the old school. He could not have been more charming.

I have always remembered an observation Peploe made

when he was visiting us at Croft House. We were looking at a picture in the hall painted by another Scottish artist who did not belong to the group. I asked Peploe if he liked it. He looked thoughtful and replied, 'A living artist can never really genuinely appreciate the work of another living artist, for he always thinks that he paints better than the other man.' That truthful and forthright reply was typical of S. J. P.

Hunter made no bones about his own capabilities, for he asserted one day to my astonishment and even to my indignation that there was no artist living at that time who was painting as well as he was. Hunter always maintained that he was not painting for today but for fifty years hence, and that although his pictures might look garish today in fifty years they would have mellowed and become beautiful in tone. Having lived twenty-five years with several of them I find that Hunter's prophecy is coming true.

To each of these three fine artists I owe a debt of gratitude which can never be repaid, for it is to them as well as to my two partners that I owe what knowledge I may have of the qualities which, collectively, make a work of art.

THE END

Index

Adam, P. W. 81

Aitken, Robert 97

Aitken Dott 38, 39, 40, 54, 56, 59, 61, 86, 105, 110

Alexander, Professor Samuel, quoted 27

Alison, David 81

Allan, David 20, 24

American opinion of Scottish Art 24, 61

Argyll, Duke of 73, 122, 125

Art, Scottish 2–4. See also under Scottish Tradition

Art Appreciation 5, 9–12, 17

Art dealers, artists' indebtedness to 37–40

Art histories 16, 17

Art in Painting, The, quoted 46

Art in Scotland 11

Art literature, dearth of 3, 7, 8

Art Schools 20

Arts in Scotland, The 26

Auld Alliance, The 19

Artist, The 63

Bailie, The, quoted 102

Baldwin Brown, Professor, quoted 30, 31

Barnes, Dr A. C., quoted 46

Barra 50

Bear, Telfer 62

Beaumont, Sir George 36

Bell, Clive 60

Berenson, Bernhard 28*n*, 36

Berkeley, Bishop, quoted 10

Blind Fiddler, The 21

Blind Man's Buff 21

Bliss, Douglas Percy 31

Boileau, Mary Hamilton, Cadell's mother 73, 75

Boswell, James, *Life of Johnson*, quoted 18, 19

Bough, Samuel 25, 26

Bouguereau, Adolphe William 53, 63

Bourdelle, Antoine 58

Boussod & Valadon 37

Boy David, The 78

Braque, Georges 58, 104

Bridie, James 105

Brough, Robert 48

Brown, Oliver 62

Bryce, Professor, quoted 18

Buchan, John 79

Buchan, Mrs John 80

Bullock's monograph on Jamesone 17

Burgess, Gelett 97

Burlington House 21, 42

Burney, Dr 18

Burns, Robert 11, 23

Cadell, Colonel A. P. H. 73

Cadell, F. C. B. 11, 17, 33, 65, 68, 73–91, 120, 121, 123, 124, 125

— academic recognition 85, 86

— and use of colour 43

— anecdotes 77–80

— attitude to art 88, 90, 91

— characteristics 76

— Classicist-Romanticist 45

— criticism 4

— early career 74–5

— exhibitions 39, 42, 61, 62, 81, 86, 105, 106

— family background 73

— France (appreciation in) 42 ; (visits to) 75, 77

— indebtedness to art dealers 37–40

— influences affecting 15–16, 36, 75

— Iona 29, 77, 78, 90

— *Jack and Tommy* 75

— London and 1, 2

— Peploe and 66

Cadell, F. C. B., Royal Academy 41
— Royal Scottish Academy 41, 85, 86
— Society of Eight 81, 82
Cadell, Dr Francis 73, 75
Cadell, Jean, 73, 75, 78, 86, 90, 125
Cadell, John. See Clark, John Percival
Cadell, Mrs. See Boileau, Mary Hamilton
Cadenhead, James 81
California, Hunter's connection with 97–8
Californian Society of Artists 98
Calvinism, effect on Scottish art 13
Campbell, Lady George 73
Cardinals, Priests and Roman Citizens Washing the Pilgrims' Feet 24
Carlyle, Thomas 63 ; portrait of 34
Cassis, Peploe and 57, 62, 63
Caw, Sir James 8, 16, 29, 41, 42, 55, 69
Celtic art 14, 15
Cézanne, Paul 11, 12, 36, 43, 45, 52, 103, 104, 106
Chambers's Journal 96
Chambers, Robert 96
Chantrey, Sir Francis Legatt 96
Chantrey Bequest 22
Chardin, Jean Baptiste Siméon 36, 52
Clark, John Percival 79
Clark, Mrs Percival. See Cadell, Jean
Classicism 45
Claude Lorrain 36
Cochran, C. B. 113
Coleridge, quoted 81
Collegiate School, Edinburgh 47, 63
Colour, constructive use of 43
Colour preference of artists 21
Colourist, description of the term 35
Colquhoun, Sir Iain 84
Colquhoun Robert 2
Common-Sense school of art 10
Comrie, Peploe at 55
Constable, John 27, 28, 33, 35, 36, 37, 64, 86, 88, 102
Continental influence on Scottish artists 15, 18, 34

Corot, Jean-Baptiste Camille 28
Cottages in Fife 119
Cottar's Saturday Night, The 24
Cowan, J. J. 89
Crawhall, Joseph 30, 33
Criticism in Art 4, 5
Croce, Benedetto, quoted 14
Crome, John 31
Crozier, William 43
Cunningham, Alan 8
Cursiter, Stanley, 4, 8, 12, 16, 18, 20, 39, 42, 54, 66 ; quoted 21

Dante 11
Daubigny, Charles François 35
Davidson, Jo 57
Declaration of Arbroath 6, 7
Degas, H. G. E. 104, 120
Delacroix, Ferdinand 27
Derain, André 58
Dialogues on Taste 18
Diaz de la Pena, N. V. 35
Doig, Wilson & Wheatly 87
Domestic painters 23, 24
Dott, P. McOmish 39, 44 ; and Peploe's new style 59
Dufy, Raoul 32
Duncan, John 81, 89
Dunlop, R. O. 62
Dutch painting, influence on Scottish art 12, 17, 22, 24, 51, 53

Edinburgh Trustees' Academy 20
Educational Methods in Art 5–7
Eliot, T. S. 26
Epstein, Jacob 84
'Expressionism' 31, 32, 34

Faure, Félix 77, 78
Ferguson, W. G. 17
Fergusson, J. D. 36–7, 42, 48, 53, 54, 57, 58, 60, 61, 62, 74, 83, 104, 105, 106, 108
Fifeshire Landscape 120
Finlay, Ian 8, 11, 12
Flemish artists, influence of 17
Ford, Sir Patrick 75, 78
Forest, Robert 96
Foulis, Robert and Andrew 20
France, Cadell in 75, 77 ; Hunter

in 103, 107, 109–10 ; Peploe in 57–8
French painting, influence on Scottish art 12, 16, 18, 19, 36, 53, 58
French relations with Scotland 19, 42
Friesz, Othon 58
Fry, Roger 22, 56, 60, 62, 88, 105
Fuseli, Henry 20

Gainsborough, Thomas 83
Galloway Landscape 30, 31
Gauguin, Paul 103
Geddes, Andrew 21, 26
Genesis 84
genre painting 22, 25
Gillies, W. G. 81
Girl Bathing, Kintyre 28
Glasgow Art Academy, eighteenth century 20
Glasgow Art Club 99, 107, 111
Glasgow Art Gallery 7, 17, 24
Glasgow Institute. See Royal Institute of Fine Arts, Glasgow
Glasgow School of Artists 2, 8, 29–34, 35, 37, 38, 43, 52, 55, 74
Goethe, Johann Wolfgang von 11
Goldsmith, Oliver 18
Grafton Galleries, London 55
Graphic 99

Hals, Franz 37 ; influence on Peploe 52
Harrison, Ion 75, 83, 84, 85, 86, 90, 104, 112, 119–26
Harvey, Sir John Martin 125
Head of a Woman 42
Hebrides, Peploe's visits to 48, 49, 50–1
Henry V 19
Henry, George 30, 31, 32
Hogarth, William 18 ; quoted 96
Holmes, Sir Charles 35
Hornel, Edward A. 30, 32, 52
Hunter, John 95
Hunter, Leslie 8, 11–12, 34, 36, 68, 75, 77, 80, 91, 123, 124, 126
— America 108
— Cadell's estimate 67
— California 97–8

Hunter, Leslie, criticism 4
— dealers' support 37–40, 82
— early career 97–9
— exhibitions 42–3, 61, 62, 102, 105, 106, 108, 109, 113
— family background 95–8
— France 103, 105, 106, 107, 109–11
— health 109, 114
— influences affecting 15–16, 36
— Loch Lomond 106, 113
— London 1, 2
— Peploe's estimate 67
— personal appearance 89
— Romanticist painter 44, 45
— signs of poverty 100
— use of colour 43
— War 1914–18 101
Hunter, William (father of Leslie Hunter) 88, 89, 90, 91
Hunter, William 18, 95
Hunter, W. G. 89, 92
Hunterian Museum 18, 88
Hutcheson, Professor 16
Huyssing, Hans 18

Impressionists 11, 27, 53, 55
Introducing Leslie Hunter 95, 115
Investigator 18
Iona 29, 40 ; Peploe in Iona 66 ; Cadell in Iona 29, 77, 78, 81, 90, 97
Irving, Sir Henry 125
Irving, H. B. 125
Irwin, William 97, 108
Italian painting 12

Jack and Tommy 75
James, Henry 53
Jamesone, George 17
Japanese painters 32
John, Augustus 105
Johnson, Dr 19
Johnston, Rt. Hon. Thomas 6
Julien's, Paris 48, 53, 63, 75
Justice, Matthew 104

Kay and Reid 38
King, Jessie 57
Kokoscha, Oscar 4
Knox, John—statue in Glasgow 96

La Torrie 57
Lavery, John 31, 81, 85
Lefevre Gallery 38
Leicester Gallery, London 61, 62, 105, 106
' Les Fauves ' 58, 103
Leslie, C. R., biographer of Constable 27, 35
Lessing, Gotthold Ephraim 16
Lewis, Wyndham 58
Leyden, Arthur 109
Lindsay, Principal 73
Lintott, H. J. 81
Listener, The 31, 42
London, the centre of British Art 1, 2
— exhibitions in 21, 26, 42, 43
London, Jack 97
Louvre 21
Lumisden, Andrew 16
Luxembourg 34, 51

MacBryde, Robert 2
McColl, D. S. 28
McDiarmid, Hugh, quoted 11
Macdonald, Duncan, 39–40, 41, 61, 63, 83, 85, 107, 114
Macdonald, Ramsay 62
Macfarlane, Mrs Jeanie 99, 100, 110, 114
McGlashan, Archibald 81
Macgregor, W. Y. 4, 15, 30, 34, 43, 81
McInnes, William 104, 109, 121
Mackay, Miss Margaret 56, 57, 58, 59
Mackay, W. D. 6 ; quoted 16
Mackie, Charles 64
McNab, The 112
McNair, William 104, 121
McTaggart, William 15, 26, 27–9, 30, 38, 52, 103
Manet, Edouard 36, 42, 55
Mann, Harrington 81
Mansfield, Katherine 57
Marriott, Charles 42 ; quoted, 60
Matisse, Henri 58, 67, 104
Mavor, Dr O. H. 112
Melville, Arthur 16, 30, 33, 34, 74, 75

Meredith, George 53
Michelangelo 74, 88, 89
Miller, Jacquin 97
Milton, John 11
Modern Masterpieces 30
Modern Movements in Painting, quoted 58
Modern Painters 51
Modern Scottish Painting, quoted 74
Mona Lisa, Pater's essay on 53
Monet, Cluade 27, 55, 104
Monticelli, A. J. T. 32
Moore, George 53
Morland, George 22
Morton, Corsan 43
Mother, The 34
Mousehold Heath 31
Munnings, Sir Alfred 9, 10
Murdoch, Blackie 42
Murry, Middleton 57

National art 14
National Gallery, Edinburgh 51, 90
National schools of art, grouping criticised 15
New English Art Club 34
New York, Peploe exhibits in 62
New York Times, quoted 108–9
Northumberland, Duke of 122
Notestein, Professor Wallace 24

Œuvre, l' 53
Orchardson, Sir W. Q. 29
Originality and plagiarism in Scottish Art 43, 44, 45
Ostade, Adrian 22

Pall Mall Magazine 99
Paris, exhibitions in 42, 56, 62, 113 ; Peploe in 57, 58
Park, Stuart 32
Pascin, Jules 58
Pater, Walter 53
Paterson, James 64, 81
Pearson & Westergaard 87
Peintres Ecossais, Les 37, 40
Peploe 12, 39
Peploe, James 49
Peploe, Mrs. See Mackay, Margaret
Peploe, Robert Luff 49

Peploe, S. J. 8, 10, 17, 34, 44, 47–70, 73, 76, 77, 88, 89, 90, 91, 104, 107, 119, 120, 121, 123, 124, 125
— academic recognition 40–1, 64, 65, 66, 81–2
— American opinion 61
— approach to painting 60, 67, 68
— Caw, Sir James, quoted 41
— change in style 44, 58–9
— Classicist painter 45
— constructive use of colour 43
— criticism 4, 41–2
— early career 47, 48
— exhibitions 38–9, 42–3, 52, 54, 55, 59, 61, 62, 63, 64, 105, 106
— France 57–8
— friendship with Cadell 64
— influences affecting 15–16, 36, 45, 52, 58
— Iona 29, 78
— London 1, 2
— marriage 56
— newspaper comments 11, 12
— Sickert's estimate 62
— teaching in Edinburgh College of Art 67
Peploe, William 47, 48
Pettie, John 29
Picasso, Pablo 58
Pink Azalea 120
Pink Rose Picture 119
Pissarro, Camille 27, 36, 41
Plagiarism in art 43–5
Porter, Dr Frederick 55, 56
Post-impressionism, 57, 58, 59, 75, 103
Pre-Raphaelites 31
Proudfoot, George 39, 40, 63
Publicity in art 41–2
Puritanical scale of values 12–13

Raeburn, Sir Henry 2, 8, 20, 22, 24, 26, 83, 112
Raeburn, Sir William 123
Railroad Monthly 98
Ramsay, Allan 2, 8, 13, 16, 17, 18, 19, 26
Reading of the Will, The 21

Reformation, The 13
Reid, A. J. McNeill 40, 83, 105, 107, 110
Reid, Alexander 37, 38, 54, 61, 63, 101, 104, 110, 114, 119
Reid (& Lefevre) 38, 64, 69, 83, 84, 87, 105, 113, 119
Reid, Thomas, quoted 10
Religion, effect on art 13
Rembrandt 21, 22
Ressich, John 42, 59, 108
Reynolds, Sir Joshua 9, 18, 19, 20
Rice, Anne 57
Richards, Grant 75
Robertson, R. C. 48
Roche, Alexander 31, 33, 52
Roffy, the poet 57
Romanticism 45
Rome, influence on Scottish art 18, 20
Rose, Robert T. 65, 66
Rothesay 95, 97
Royal Academy 9, 18, 20, 25, 26, 41, 81, 86
Royal Institute of Fine Arts, Glasgow 37, 41, 54, 69, 81, 86, 123
Royal Scottish Academy 16, 30, 40, 41, 51, 54, 55, 64, 65, 69, 74, 81, 86
Rubens, Peter Paul 36
Runciman, Alexander 20
Ruskin, John 22, 63
Russian Ballet in Paris 57
Rutter, Frank 30, 42

Sadler, Michael 57
St Luke's Academy, Edinburgh 18, 20
St Martin's Lane Academy, London 18
Salon d'Automne Exhibition, Paris 58
Sargent, John Singer 32
Schnabel, Arthur 87
Scot in History, The, quoted 24
Scott Lauder School 29
Scotsman, The, quoted 6, 11, 12, 87, 106
Scott, David 25
Scott, Sir Walter 23

INDEX

Scottish Art 18, 42. See also Scottish National Art; Scottish Tradition

Scottish Art Exhibitions in London 21, 26, 42, 43

Scottish Art Historians 16, 17

Scottish Art Review 33–5

Scottish Nationalism 2–4

Scottish National Art Characteristics 14, 15, 16

Scottish Painters Exhibition, Burlington House, 1939 21

Scottish Painting, quoted 41

Scottish School of Philosophy 10

Scottish Tradition in Art 12–35; Puritanical scale of values 12–13; national characteristics 14–16; The Historians 16; The Artists 17; Jamesone 17; Allan Ramsay 18; The Auld Alliance 19; The Art schools 20; Sir Henry Raeburn 20; Sir David Wilkie 21; The Domestic Scene 23; American opinion 24; William McTaggart 26–9; The Glasgow School 29–30; The 'Galloway Landscape' 30; 'Expressionism' 31; *Scottish Art Review* 33–5

Scougalls, The 17

Segonzac, Dunoyer de 4

Service, G. W. 90, 122

Seurat, Georges 104

Sickert, W. R. 62, 106

Sinclair, A. G. 81

Sisley, Alfred 27, 41

Skye 51

Smith, Joan 109, 110

Société des Beaux Arts 38

Society of Eight 66, 81, 82

Society of Scottish Artists 54, 86, 88

Spangled Cock, The 33

Spanish painting 12

Steer, Wilson 27, 28

Stevenson, Macaulay 31, 34

Storey, Principal 73

Storm Seascape, the North End, Iona 119

Sunset Magazine 98

Symons, Arthur 53

Tassie, James 20

Tate Gallery 102

Tattersall, John 104

Taylor, E. A. 57, 69, 101

Taylor, Francis Henry 9

Teniers, David 22

Thomson, Rev. John 24–5

Times Literary Supplement, quoted 12

Tonge, John 26

Turner, J. M. W. 25, 27

Tweedsmuir, Lord. See Buchan, John

Tyrell, Lord 62

Van Dyck, Sir Anthony 21

Van Gogh, Theo 35, 37

Van Gogh, Vincent 103

Vegetable Stall 4

Venetian painters 27, 35

Vuillard, J. E. 55

Walton, E. A. 30, 33

Warnes, sculptor 96

Watson, Anne 49

Whistler 83

Whistler, J. A. McN., quoted 1, 31, 34, 40, 50, 68, 83, 99, 103

White, S. S. 103

Wilde, Oscar 28, 53

Wilkie, David 2, 8, 21–4, 26, 52

William Hunter and his Museum 18

Wilson, Richard 25

Winckelmann, Johann Joachim 16

Wintour, J. C. 25, 26

Wood, Miss 124

Wordsworth, William 28

Yale University Press 24

Zoffany, Johann 18

Zola, Emile 53